Praise for Fred Haefe[...]

REBUILDING THE [...]

"A book that will be treasured by all who long for a large wind in the hair of an otherwise circumscribed life."
—James Welch, author of *Killing Custer*

"If you'd like to listen while a funny, street-wise fellow tells the story of refinding himself in the details, *Rebuilding the Indian* is your book. I loved it!"
—Bill Kittredge, author of *Hole in the Sky*

"*Rebuilding the Indian* is as satisfying as the act of restoration it describes. The mechanical details link up like clues in a thriller, the dialogue is funny and dead-on, and the characters—Harley riders in leather pillbox hats, parts-shop scavengers, friends, bystanders, skeptical wives—are all alive on the page. Haefele's rebuilding of the Indian and of himself is an inspiring story."
—Ian Frazier, author of *Family* and *Coyote vs. Acme*

"This remembrance of turning a box of junk into a gleaming 1941 Indian Chief has a universal roar. . . . Just the right mix of gearhead details and personal reflections."
—*USA Today*

"The tale of woe turns to *whoah* at the end of 210 pages as his beloved old machine hits the road."
—*New York Post*

"Haefele's enthusiasm and carefully crafted writing draw you in from the start . . . you'll want to feel the wind in your hair—heck, even the bugs in your teeth."
—*MAXIM*

"This is a strange world Haefele takes you into, one that teeters on the edge between the mundane and the bizarre."
—*The Missoulian*

"*Rebuilding the Indian* reminds me of the best parts of one of my favorite books, *Zen and the Art of Motorcycle Maintenance*. But in many ways Haefele's book is less troubled and more mature: less about the dark caverns of the intellect and more about the joy the eye takes in the perfect arch of a polished fender, less about tangled philosophy and more about the wisdom the hand discovers following the shining orbs of a reground crankshaft."
—James Crumley, author of *The Last Good Kiss*

"What Haefele writes about wonderfully, in his mellow, understated way, is how the Indian project became a test of his love and resolve."
—*Esquire*

"Haefele describes how his search for vintage parts eventually involved an entire community of fanatical mechanics, impoverished motorcycle collectors, and renegade bikers—a collaboration, he realizes, that gave him skills as much social and spiritual as practical."
—*The New Yorker*

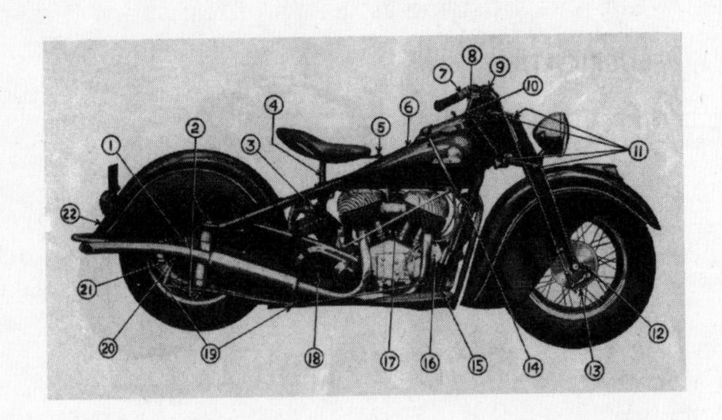

Riverhead Books

NEW YORK

REBUILDING THE *Indian*

A Memoir

Fred Haefele

RIVERHEAD BOOKS
Published by The Berkley Publishing Group
A division of Penguin Putnam Inc.
375 Hudson Street
New York, New York 10014

The author gratefully acknowledges permission to reprint lines from "Under the Maud Moon," from *The Book of Nightmares* by Galway Kinnell. Copyright © 1971 by Galway Kinnell. Reprinted by permission of Houghton Mifflin Co. All rights reserved.

Book design by Deborah Kerner
Cover design by Kiley Thompson

First Riverhead hardcover edition: June 1998
First Riverhead trade paperback edition: June 1999
Riverhead trade paperback ISBN: 1-57322-734-X

The Penguin Putnam Inc. World Wide Web site address is
http://www.penguinputnam.com

The Library of Congress has catalogued the Riverhead hardcover edition as follows:

Haefele, Fred.
Rebuilding the Indian : a memoir / by Fred Haefele.
p. cm.
ISBN 1-57322-099-X (acid-free paper)
1. Haefele, Fred. 2. Motorcyclists—United States—Biography.
3. Indian motorcycle—Maintenance and repair. I. Title.
GV1060.2.H24A3 1998 97-51344 CIP
629.227'5'092—dc21

Printed in the United States of America

10 9 8 7 6 5 4 3 2 1

ACKNOWLEDGMENTS

A thousand thanks for everyone who helped me, but especially for Magoo, Ronnie and Bummy, Shane and Kevin, Sneezy and Speedstick, for Rick and Frankie and Cowboy Bob, for Dee, Craig, Bootsy, Neil and Bryan, Kim, and of course, Yvonne and Chaz. Thanks, too, for all the technical support and free advice I got from Ken, from Michael Breeding, and last, from Frank at Starklite Cycles, for whom there was no such thing as a stupid question.

For

Caroline

and

Phoebe,

for

K *and* S

LUBRICATION CHART

1. **Rear Hub and Brake Drum Bearings**—Grease every 1,000 miles. **Note:** Brake Drum fitting is between hub and drum, remove wheel to locate.
2. **Spring Frame Units**—Grease every 1000 miles.
3. **Generator**—Few drops of light oil at oilers at each end of generator every 1500 miles—See Care of Generator.
4. **Seat Post**—Grease every 1000 miles.
5. **Saddle Front Connection**—Grease very lightly every 500 miles.
6. **Air Cleaner Element**—(Air cleaner on left side on carburetor)—Remove element, dip clean in gasoline and allow to dry. Dip in 10W engine oil and allow to drain—reinstall. Service every month or 1000 miles for normal use; oftener if motorcycle is operated in extreme climates or under conditions of extreme dirt.
7. **Handlebar Control Grips**—Unscrew protector sleeves and apply a few drops of light oil every 1000 miles.
8. **Hand Brake Lever and Cable**—Oil lever pivot and cable every 500 miles.
9. **Controls**—Apply few drops of light oil at upper ends inside covering once each week.
10. **Upper and Lower Head Bearing**—Repack with high melting point grease every 10,000 miles. Lower bearing has alemite fitting on left side.

11. **Fork**—Lubricated by fork fluid. Maintain proper level only.
12. **Speedometer Drive**—Grease every 1,000 miles.
13. **Front Brake Cam Needle Bearing**—Clean and pack with fresh grease every 6000 miles.
14. **Front Hub and Brake Drum Bearings**—Grease every 1000 miles.
15. **Shift Lever**—Oil every 500 miles.
16. **Brake and Clutch Pedals**—(Clutch pedal on left side)—Grease every 1000 miles.
17. **Distributor**—Grease lightly every 1000 miles.
18. **Footstarter Segment and Shaft**—Oil every 500 miles.
19. **Footstarter Crank**—Grease every 1000 miles.
20. **Brake and Clutch Rod Clevises**—(Clutch rod on left side)—Apply a few drops of oil to front and rear clevis pins every 1000 miles.
21. **Rear Brake Cam Bearing**—Grease every 1000 miles.
22. **Chain**—See Care and Adjustment of Chain.

CHAPTER 1

PARTS FATHERS

"Drop by the garage sometime.
I'll show you my pile." CHAZ

ONCE UPON A TIME IN THE PACIFIC NORTHWEST, THERE LIVED a handsome young biker named Benny. One afternoon in early fall, Benny was out burning highway on his '53 Harley Panhead, and somewhere north of Corvallis, he stopped at a roadhouse for refreshment.

The only customer in the place was an old farmer, drinking by himself at the bar. The two men struck up a conversation, and before long they were talking motorcycles. When Benny mentioned he was restoring a '46 Indian Chief, the old man's eyes lit up. He cocked his head and fixed Benny with a peculiar stare that made the young biker uneasy. The farmer made a veiled reference to some old junk he had squirreled away in his barn, then summoned the bartender and bought another round.

The hour grew late. It began to rain. The farmer suggested Benny sleep at his place, a few miles up the road. Benny followed the old man's pickup on his bike but soon lost the taillights in heavy fog. Benny throttled back, pulled over at a crossroads, and swore. With zero visibility and the rain pounding down, he rolled his Panhead into a dilapidated barn by the roadside, spread his sleeping bag out on the hard dirt floor, and fell quickly into a deep, dreamless sleep.

The next morning, sunlight streamed through the cracks of the barn and Benny rose, bleary-eyed and hungover, to find himself in a fabulous place. Every rafter, loft, stall, and stanchion in that barn was crammed with Indian motorcycle parts: Chief frames and Scout fenders, connecting rods, flywheels, gas tanks and engine cases, pistons, seats and kickers, forks and sprockets. Benny looked around in wonder. He knew very well what had happened: He'd had the sheer dumb luck to stumble onto every biker's mother lode: the Lost City of Parts.

The enchanted barn, the mysterious farmer, the great cache of motorcycle parts (all made in the United States)—there are dozens of variations to this story. Some of them have about them this fairy-tale quality, some of them don't, and yet they all feature wily but beneficent old men in the role of gatekeeper.

In the lives of most cyclists, parts are a driving force, a common currency, a lingua franca. The search for a '41 Chief shift lever is the reason for late-night trips to bars, for dozens of long-distance calls, the reason for combing through junkyards, garages, and chicken coops. Parts are a never-ending quest. They are the fever and the cure, the question and the answer, the reason for road trips that transcend time lines and even international boundaries.

Parts are the reason I'm here at the county fairgrounds this gorgeous spring evening in Missoula, Montana. These American Motorcyclist Association (AMA) flat-track races are the first I've attended in more than twenty years. Flanked by snowcapped mountains, this small university town at the confluence of three rivers looks green and fresh.

After a long, dreary winter, Missoula on a spring night looks about as good as it's ever going to get.

I'm here shopping for an Indian basketcase. An *Indian* is a make of motorcycle, defunct since 1953. A *basketcase* is biker argot for a quantity of parts that, when bolted together, comprise the greater part of a motorcycle. My reason is simple: I'm a fifty-one-year-old tree surgeon, an ex-professor with an unsuccessful novel under my belt. It took me six years to write my novel, four years not to sell it. I've come into $5,000 dollars and I'm in the mood to do something foolish.

I've been shopping for about a month now, thumbing through magazines like *Wallneck's, Hemmings Motor News,* and *Old Bike Journal.* I've responded to ads around the country and I've hit what, for enthusiasts, must be a familiar wall: There is no real way to tell what you're buying—or whom you're buying it from—unless you go to see it. And for most of us, flying around the country to simply *look* at project bikes is out of the question.

But in a couple months of phone inquiries, I've garnered this much information:

1. If you're determined to buy an Indian, buy a Chief. Indian manufactured this big 74ci V-twin for better than twenty years. So parts are relatively easy to come by and they're mostly interchangeable.

2. Learn to accept the "5-10 Law": If you buy a Chief basketcase for $5,000, you will end up putting another $10,000 into it, no matter how you try to scrimp.

3. Whatever you do, don't buy a basketcase. They are pigs in pokes. They will break your heart. They will drive you mad.

I've heard that a local biker and collector known as Chaz may have a Chief basketcase to sell, but he doesn't return calls and seems skittish when I do get him on the phone. So when I hear Chaz is racing tonight, I decide to come down for a look.

There's a line of Harleys out in front of the grandstands that must be forty bikes long. Although I can tell a Sportster from a DuoGlide, I know even less about Harleys than I do Indians. Harleys were always too big, heavy, and chromey for my tastes. I liked the sleeker, cleaner lines of the old British vertical twins. But since a Harley is the V-twin all-American blood brother to the Indian, I try to look at them with an open mind.

The biker crowd is incredibly exotic, distracting—so many winged tattoos, so many ferocious-looking eagles on so many fat guys' T-shirts. They wear so much metal, they actually clink when they walk past. And never would you imagine, outside of a Bergman movie or the Oakland Raiders' locker room, that on a beautiful May evening you'd see so many people dressed in black.

From the infield, you can hear the bikes rap out as the tuners make their last-minute adjustments. These motors sound familiar to me. They don't have the high-revving, killer-bee pitch of the Japanese multicylinders. Instead, there is the mellow, resonant baritone note of the British vertical twin I used to own, back in 1969.

When the motorcycles roll up to the line, I'm startled to see that they *are,* for the most part, those British twins: Triumphs, BSAs, and Nortons, bikes that have been out of production for twenty or thirty years, the same motorcycles I knew back in the '60s. Later on, I learn that this is because the power pulse (usable horsepower) the space-age multicylinders produce is unsuited to the off-and-on traction of dirt-track racing.

I watch the British bikes take their practice laps and then a gaggle of 1940s domestic handshifters approaches the line. This is a special old-timer class. The bikes are out of the '40s and '50s, mostly American V-twins, though there is an Ariel and an older Norton, too. Their riders appear loose, jocular. They have a kind of recreational look about them, and as they rev their motors and approach the starting line, I try to figure out which one might be Chaz. Is it the rider in the pudding bowl–style helmet with a cigar in his teeth? The rider with the skewbald gas tank with the word "Parts" written on the side in Magic Marker? Or is it the entry with a Bird of Paradise Hawaiian shirt over his leathers?

At the last minute, a rider with an ash-blond ponytail rolls up to the line on a cherry-red hand-shift Harley. His bike nearly stalls out, and to keep it lit he zips off in the opposite direction, horses the machine around and back to the line. Then they are off. There is a colossal rooster tail of dust and the smell of Castrol. A ragged wall of noise erupts from the straight-piped V-twin motors that is so powerful I can feel it, smell it, almost *see* it.

I call Chaz a couple days later. "So which one was *you*?" I ask.

"I was the guy with the ponytail," he says, "riding the red Harley." He seems flattered I caught his race.

I tell him there was so much dust I couldn't see how he finished.

He laughs and says, "I finished dead middle."

Before I went to Chaz's garage, I'd inspected one other local basketcase. This was a '48 Chief that belonged to a biker known as "Bootsy."

Bootsy's place is in the Rattlesnake Creek drainage, a couple miles north of town. It looks like a gentleman's ranch: late-model pickups, whitewashed corral, one barn for the horses and one barn for the bikes. Bootsy himself is in his forties, with a wire-bristled beard, a round moon face, and spectacles. As it happens, on race night Bootsy ran in the same heat as Chaz, but I hadn't identified him, either.

I couldn't help but recall Rule #3 (Whatever you do, don't buy a basketcase) when I saw Bootsy's pile. If this advice was true for the enthusiast, it must go double for a novice like myself. In an entire box of parts Bootsy showed me, the only thing I could positively identify was a cylinder barrel. And even then, I couldn't be sure what *kind* of cylinder: Was it really from a '48? Was it really from a Chief? Was it even from an Indian?

Later on, I asked a biker acquaintance known as Dirty Dick about Bootsy. Dirty Dick had one thing to say: "Oh no, man. *No*. You don't wanna buy from *that* guy. Bootsy will sell you junk."

I've heard the same thing about virtually every other dealer in vintage bikes, and I've decided that this is probably because most of this stuff *is* junk, and a decade ago it probably would have been hauled off to the scrap works without a second thought.

I first heard about Chaz on the night I decided to take on this project. I was sitting in a bar called the Missoula Club, a run-down sports bar in the center of town. It was a Friday night, and as the chatter about my project spilled out from a small knot of friends and into the crowd, an odd thing began to happen. Friends and strangers alike came up to hand me scraps of paper with phone numbers on them. "You've got to call this guy," they would say. "He knows *every*thing about Indians." When I finally left the bar, I had a half-dozen slips of paper, all of them with Chaz's number.

Chaz's garage is on the North Side of town. I've always been partial to the North Side. It's a real blue-collar neighborhood, no frills. No sidewalks in most places, either. There are mailboxes at the curbs—where there are curbs—and there is lots of stuff out in people's yards: Boats. Appliances. Every kind of car. Some old beetles, but mostly Detroit iron, missing hoods and doors. Vintage pickups and old muscle cars, gone to lard. Elaborate vegetable gardens. Firewood stacked in ricks, antlers over the doorjambs.

In front of Chaz's garage are a dozen or more bikes under a large rain-soaked tarp. By and large, this is where he keeps the imports. But inside—*inside* is where he keeps the good stuff.

Hanging on the wall is a photo of an old-time shop in Carnal, Kentucky, with a gas pump out front. It bears a sign that says "Carnal Garage," and I'm never able to think of Chaz's shop again without thinking of that name: The walls and ceilings are hung with every kind of gasket, fender, gas tank, handlebar, and frame. Bikes are predominant, but there are enough electric guitars, hunting rifles, exotic tools, and even lawn mowers to make you think you've wandered into some kind of shade-tree hockshop by mistake. Among the rarities are the red WR Harley, the flat-track racer I saw in action (the one with the Four Roses hand-shifter knob), a 1940 Indian Rainbow Chief, a '48 Indian Daytona Big Base Scout (according to Chaz, the mount of that legendary Indian racer Bobby Hill), and perhaps the most prized, a 1939 Harley-Davidson Knucklehead. An old farmer in Dutton led Chaz to it after it sat in a pasture for some forty years. There is also a little Mustang Pony with a spectacular flaming paint job and a huge V-twin motor that dwarfs the scooter's tiny frame.

I ask Chaz, "Whose bike is that?"

He beams. "That's Honey Bunny's cycle," he says. "I built that specially for my little daughter, Willa."

The place is wondrously distracting, even intoxicating. Put simply, I want to buy, ride, or fondle everything in that shop. What's more, there's something about the careless pack-rat disarray that suggests Chaz might not know exactly what he has, and this apparent carelessness might work to my advantage.

This impression gives way very quickly to the conviction that he certainly *does* know what he has, and that I am in the process of being read like a book, played like a fiddle. In the end, probably nobody has ever been more at the mercy of a crafty purveyor of vintage cycles than I am the first time I set foot in this Cave of Ali Baba, Chaz's garage.

Chaz is thick-armed, stocky, remarkably tattoo-free for being in the business as long as he's been. He is never without his black Indian motorcycle cap, and except for the ponytail that hangs down well past his shoulders, with his granny glasses and his round, serious face, he looks every bit the son of a Scandinavian wheat farmer from the hinterlands of eastern Montana—which in fact, he is.

Chaz does voices: a kind of inner-city falsetto, a Zap Comics–style pirate captain that never sounds quite right, and a passable sourdough old-timer. Chaz is insulted that I mistake this voice for Walter Brennan, when it's actually an obscure character actor named Royal Dano, who specializes in camp cooks, prospectors, and crusty barflies.

In short order I find out a couple of things about Chaz: He feels embattled, *invaded,* because both Harleys and Indians, the classic American V-twins, long the blue-collar worker's bike of choice, have now been discovered by yuppies. As the demand for them goes up, the prices skyrocket. Dealers from all over the world (in particular a tribe of rapacious Australians) regularly scour the countryside for vintage bikes and parts, in much the same way, according to Chaz, that the great Russian trawlers routinely strip the Great Banks of fish. Harley-Davidsons now seem featured in every other fashion shoot. Movie stars ride them, and they appear regularly in such high-end magazines as *Cigar Aficionado* and *Mercedes-Benz.* With undisguised contempt, Chaz refers to Harleys as "yuppie bikes," while Indian collectors are even now talking wistfully of the day, five years ago, when you could get into a Chief basketcase for only a thousand or two.

In addition to his motorcycle business, Chaz operates a hauling service, with a running ad in the local newspaper. He does this in part to supplement his motorcycle income, but mostly he does it to gain access to old garages and barns that no one else has yet picked over.

My first couple of sessions at Chaz's garage, I try to ask him all the things I need to know.

"How long does it take to restore a basketcase?"

He says, "That depends on how much money you have."

"What's the hardest aspect of the restoration?"

He says, "That depends on how much money you have."

"Should I buy the 1950 Indian Warrior vertical-twin rolling basketcase the guy in North Carolina will sell me for three thousand bucks?"

At this question, Chaz curls his lip and gives me a straight answer. "Stay away from that late-model vertical stuff," he says. "They're a fake British bike, is what they are, and they're the worst kind of junk."

It's always busy in Chaz's garage. The phone keeps ringing. He has two children, ages ten and seven, and a third child on the way. The kids are in and out constantly, and there is a kitten named Sylvie who keeps sneaking in to nap on Chaz's Sportster Cafe Racer. Bikers stop by to chat about parts, or else they bring their Harleys in for Chaz to work on, and it's not until my second visit that I actually get to see the basketcase.

The Chief is sitting in a little warren in the back of the garage, a room so crammed with stuff you literally can't turn around: an old Harmony guitar, a pressure cooker, an eight-track player, a couple of No. 7 coyote traps and a spinning rod, ceramic swordfish lamp, bins full of parts, and what looks like a motorized skateboard.

And then, suddenly, there it is—that thing I've been looking for all along: a mottled steel frame, crouching in the midst of all this debris, an engineless skeleton on a pair of rubberless rims. A gearshift lever and disarticulated clutch pedal dangle from the frame, and a pair of rusty gas tanks are fixed loosely in place. Those areas of the tanks not dinged up or peppered with the holes of abortive bodywork are painted a kind of mustard-phlegm color. Low in the hindquarters, tall in the chest, to my eyes at least the Chief stands out in this setting like a pedigree shepherd at the local pound. I know how this will sound, but when I first see that frame, I feel a little shock of recognition.

In the course of the next couple of visits, I see a little more of my basketcase each time—a generator, a seat, a set of handlebars—so that it's quite a lot like a striptease in reverse. I'm beginning to commune with that frame on some peculiar level. I *know* that frame from somewhere—its massive, overbuilt, vaguely industrial look. The chipped-up paint, the tinge of rust here and there. Finally it hits me. Particularly in this unmotorized form, the Chief closely resembles the heavy, crude-looking preplastic steel toys of the '30s and '40s, the toys stored away in the attics of my boyhood.

When Chaz rummages around on an upper shelf, then drags out a heavy valenced fender and sets it over the front wheel, I see that bulbous, rounded-off look known throughout the '40s as "the streamliner."

Like any good salesman, Chaz saves the best for last. So when it's finally time for me to see the motor, instead of pulling together a box of parts from the backroom bins, Chaz goes into his sourdough quaver, says something like "Tarnation! Now, whur'd I *put* th' dad-blamed thing?"

He disappears into yet another room, reappears dragging out not a box of parts but a fully assembled 74-cubic-inch Chief motor and transmission.

I'm pop-eyed with excitement. Whatever resistance I have to this sale has all but vanished. I check the serial number and determine by the prefix that the motor is a prewar '41. Then, in a stroke of pure sales genius, Chaz loosens the head bolts so I can peer down into the motor. I don't know precisely what I'm expecting to see, but I touch the surface of the front piston and it gives beneath my finger, making a brief, hissing sigh. My heart leaps. *It's alive!*

I'm generally hopeful about things. My basketcase is in chunks as opposed to boxes, so to some extent I can see what I'm getting. Yet at the same time, I find myself thinking that, chunks or no chunks, I am buying a $5,000 motorcycle "project" (I now use this euphemism) from a man who seems like a decent enough outlaw biker, but who, in the end, I know very little about, other than the fact he won't take checks, has an unlisted phone number and at least one alias. I decide, finally, that buying a basketcase is a lot like taking your first bungie jump, and that sooner or later you have to just go over the side and hope that everything holds. Whether he knows it or not, because I'm buying my basketcase from him Chaz will become my official mentor, my spiritual guide to the mysteries of the Indian and the V-twin engine.

There was a man they called Parts Father who lived right here in town, and he must have died just days before I attended my first swap meet in May 1995. There were leaflets with his picture all over the fairgrounds advertising a "going-away party" to be thrown in his honor, thirty miles south, down the Bitterroot River Valley.

Since Parts Father died at the advent of my Indian adventures, all I know about him is that he helped hundreds of bikers with their cycle projects. When the parts they needed couldn't be found, he fabricated them himself. In fact, he was Chaz's own guide and mentor for years. Now, six months after his death, Parts Father is already a legend, and bikers speak his name quietly and with respect.

I didn't go to Parts Father's send-off that blustery evening in early May. I heard that by nighttime the weather had turned to snow but that there were hundreds of people there anyway, friends and bikers from all over the Northwest. I heard all kinds of things about that party, including the story that they burned a Harley in his honor. I mention this to Chaz late one night, as we are returning from a parts expedition to Portland.

"Yeah," says Chaz. "Sure they burned one. But it was only a two-fifty Aeramacchi."

Chaz pauses, then says, with genuine reverence, "For Parts Father, they should have burned a *Knucklehead*."

I wake up on a cold, rainy morning in June, determined to buy. We have a quick photo session in Chaz's garage. Chaz is very accommodating and seems to know just the kind of shot I want. Perhaps he understands exactly which areas of the brain are involved in the sale of a motorcycle and why people buy motorcycles—which seems to be less about desire than need. I'm struck by how much of the pimp there seems to be in his line of business—in me, at least, motorcycles promote a particularly lurid species of desire.

Chaz takes a snapshot called "Fred with Parts," where I put my arms around that funky old motor and a friend suddenly jerks the stand away from beneath it. I now have a photo of me with my eyes bugging out, holding the engine's full weight for the first time. It's heavy as an anvil.

In the course of this I choose to ignore a couple broken cooling fins on the front cylinder head. But I also notice the fractured engine-mount casing, and it concerns me.

Chaz is reassuring; this is routine heli-arc repair. He senses I'm still dubious, and suddenly we're down on his garage floor, checking the welds on the casings of his 1940 Rainbow Chief. We can't find them.

Really, it's dark as a cave in that garage. Chaz sprays half a can of carb cleaner up there to degrease it, and we stink up the place. Soon an irate Yvonne waddles down the hallway that connects the shop to the living room. She draws herself up and demands an explanation for the stench. What's more formidable than a hugely pregnant woman wanting answers, I'm sure I wouldn't know. Gallantly, I blame myself for the stink. Chaz one-ups me by doing the same. It seems nobody wants to queer this sale. Yvonne looks skeptical. "Well," she says at last, "then you're *both* a couple of assholes."

That evening I go back to the garage to take delivery. All the way over there I tell myself why this is *The One*: Because it comes in chunks. Because the motor *spoke* to me. Because I'm tired of shopping. Because, because, because.

Someone told me to be sure the bike has a title. I ask Chaz, "By the way, is there a title?"

He gives me a surprised, faintly amused look, as if to say, "Oh. He wants a *title,* too." "Believe me," he says at last. "A title is going to be the least of your worries."

On this note, I count the fifty hundred-dollar bills I withdrew from my mad-money account onto an Electra Glide seat. Chaz counts it again, swiftly, proficiently. He tells me, by the way, he never goes to a swap meet with any less than $5,000 cash in his pockets. This may be true, but on the way to get the bill of sale notarized, he can only come up with a buck fifty for gas to put in his van. He mentions it's good that it's nearly dark out because his plates have expired. I mention that we need to move fast because my truck lights don't work. I wonder what the hell either of us is doing, buying and selling motorcycles, but I have already figured that one out: Motorcycles are somehow not of this world.

It costs seven dollars for the notarization. We've just exchanged

$5,000 in cash, yet somehow nobody seems to have any money. There's a madcap moment where, to demonstrate this, we both jerk our pockets inside out and nothing falls to the floor but pennies and lint. I've lost track of any sense of etiquette this event might demand. Determined to get on with it, I charge the notarization on an overdrawn MasterCard. This whole transaction is taking on a dreamlike quality.

Back at Chaz's garage we load the frame onto my truck bed, racing the end of the long Montana twilight. It begins to rain. I secure the frame to the rack with ropes and straps, cover it with a tarp. Then we two-man the motor out and set it on the passenger side of my truck seat. In doing this Chaz looks briefly, closely at the front jug. Then he does a voice, some kind of generic Asian patois: "Huh," he says. "Now, why someone take glinder to bloken cooling fin?"

All the way home, drivers flash their lights at me. It's quite dark by now and I take all the backstreets, rolling through stop signs, hurrying as if I'm pursued, while the tarp flaps along behind me like a raven's wings. Beside me, the old motor sits on the pickup seat, heavy as a meteor. I can smell its scent of ancient motor oil, and I'm wondering all the way home: Why *did* someone take a grinder to that broken cooling fin?

My friend Kim comes over to help me unload. We quickly horse the old Chief into the garage, take a moment to contemplate my new pile of parts sitting there on the bare concrete beneath a naked lightbulb. At last Kim says with genuine awe, "My *God,* but that thing is ugly!"

Back in the house, I look at my coffee table book full of immaculately restored Chiefs. Then I think about the pile out in my garage. I have a drink and then I go to bed. I'm wiped out from this transaction, but all night long I lie awake thinking, Boy oh boy, Fred. You've gone and done it *this* time. . . .

CHAPTER 2

TRACE ELEMENTS

For $5,000, the price of my basketcase, I could have bought a state-of-the-art warp-speed Japanese multicylinder that revs to 12,000 rpm, goes 150 miles an hour, and is made of materials like titanium and carbon-fiber plastic. It would be a computer-designed bike with interstellar styling. It would have a name like "Ninja" or "Katana," and it would be painted in neon flashfire.

For $5,000 I could even have bought a first-rate restoration of a studly British twin—a Triumph or a Norton from the early '70s, a classic bike that runs and looks terrific.

Indian fanciers tout the convenience of being able to buy most of the bike's bolts and fasteners down at the local hardware store, the electical components at the corner auto-parts dealer. And when all these parts are finally restored and pieced back together, what I will have—if I'm lucky—is a huge, side-valve ("flathead") engine whose design dates back to 1922, the infancy of the internal combustion motor. It is a machine that, according to Indian historian Jerry Hatfield, "has all the technical wizardry of old lawn mowers."

But I've become fond of the idea that the '41 motor and the '47 chassis averages out to '44, the year of my own birth (though because it will look like a '47, the machine will take that designation on the registration). I scrape most of the original finish from the frame with an old hunting knife, one I've used to field-dress deer, and it feels odd—as if I were flensing this old steel. As I scrape and sand away particles of paint and metal from the postwar '40s, I'm never far from the idea that this machine and I both come from the same chaotic and calamitous decade, and that we must surely share trace elements of a common origin, as if we were both created from the same catastrophic Big Bang.

The Indian was conceived as the first production motorized bicycle (known then as a "motocycle") and was born in Springfield, Massachusetts, in the beginning of the twentieth century. Carl Oskar Hedstrom, the designer and engineer, and his partner, the entrepreneur George Hendee, built their motocycle along the lines of the bicycle racer's "pacing machines," and registered the trademark in 1901.

Since Hedstrom was Scandinavian, they could have called their new vehicle the "Norski." Instead of the famous war bonnet Chief on the gas tank, it could have featured a craggy-faced Viking with a great horned helmet. But the two partners were bent on a name they considered as uniquely American as their new machine, and "Indian" became their marque.

Over the next fifty years, Indian became one of the most famous motorcycles in the world. On the racetrack, the lighter, faster Scout model would set speed and endurance records that stood for decades. The larger-displacement Chief and the flagship of the line, the multicylinder Indian Four, would set standards for comfort and high-speed cruising that Harley-Davidson chased unsuccesfully for years.

But by the end of the Great Depression, out of perhaps half a dozen American manufacturers, Indian and Harley were the only two left that still produced motorcyles. And following a series of inept company heads and ill-conceived adventures into the field of outboard motors, aircraft parts, and even refrigerators, Indian was in trouble. Military contracts helped Indian survive during World War II, but after the war the company remained shaky and badly in need of new leadership. Nineteen forty-two was the last year of manufacture for both the popular Sport Scout and the legendary Indian Four. The only bike Indian continued to produce was the Chief, which, with its antiquated design, was having a hard time competing with Harley-Davidson's overhead-valve models. Under a new president, Indian gambled everything on a brand-new design, a prototype they hoped would keep up with the increasingly popular lightweight British twins. But these Indian "verticals" were rushed into production before they were ready, and proved to be a disaster from which the company never recovered. They closed their doors for good in 1953, and the Indian became an instant classic.

I was born in Detroit in May 1944, a month before D Day. My parents were Christian Scientists, so I was born at home. It's considered bad form to point these things out, but the Rh factor my mother was unaware of made my home birth a near disaster.

"You were purple as a plum," Mom told me cheerfully, giving me that little we-sure-beat-the-odds-that-time head wag of hers.

Detroit is a kind of free-fire zone now, but from the '40s through the '50s, it was a vital and prosperous place. There was a sense that in manufacturing motorized vehicles—or even being associated with making them, since my father worked for a bank—we were all involved in something tremendously important. When the president of General

Motors said that "what's good for GM is good for the country," this seemed to us like plain good sense.

In addition to automobiles, the name "Michigan" still evoked images of pristine forests and rivers. Even while it used its lakes for dump sites, the state called itself "Water Wonderland," and as a boy I believed that, somewhere beyond the pale of the industrial south, Michigan was still a wild and primitive place where trappers and Indians roamed.

In 1948, my father took a job in Flint, and I grew up on a small "gentleman's farm" just south of the city. I had a distant father, a reclusive older brother. I had what Orwell described as "the lonely child's habit of making up stories about myself," and I would follow a small creek into the woods behind our house, watching the light shift through the hardwood canopy. I spent hundreds, maybe thousands of hours back there, and to this day the sound of the wind seems like a sound track for my childhood.

Throughout those years I had a vivid, recurring dream: I would flash along, inches above the ground, at incredible rates of speed, but perfectly in control. The sensation was like flowing water, but it could suddenly turn into flight. This sensation was a thing of both the body and the spirit, and I would wake up spellbound, exhilarated. *Alive.*

On North Saginaw Avenue in Flint, circa 1953, there was an Indian Motorcycle shop, and in the parking lot there was a sign that said: "Harley riders, don't park your bikes *here.*" The Harley–Indian rivalry was serious back then, and partisans often came to blows. There were rough-looking men hanging around that lot, smoking and spitting. The engineer boots and leather jackets with the lightning slash of zippers is now clichéd, but at the time it was unnerving. Many of these men were vets who had come back from overseas and, like their counterparts twenty years later, simply gave up trying to resume their lives where they left off. All they had left was their restlessness. These were men, I now recognize, who did not want a lot: a job that paid the bills, a good machine, cheap gas, and plenty of highway to burn. These were men I would end up having a lot more in common with than I thought.

At the age of nine, at roughly the same time the Indian Motorcyle Company was finally going under, I buried a mason jar on a hillside, beneath a tree. Inside I placed my favorite toy car, a ZagNut candy bar, and maybe a dollar in loose change. Even then I knew I was burying a time capsule. I just had no idea for *whom*. Most likely, though, it was for someone just like me—another lonely kid who didn't like himself much.

So when we finally moved away, the first thing I did was change my name. The name I picked was Frederick—my great-grandfather's name. And the boy called "Paul"—the shy, self-doubting twelve-year-old I used to be—was to be left behind in Michigan for good. Him and his little mason jars and woodlot wanderings. When we moved away I had big plans, and Paul wasn't part of them. Somehow, I would start my life over as a different person.

The last time I owned a motorcycle was twenty-six years ago, a chrome and candy-apple British twin that was described by a 1964 *HotRod* magazine as "the fastest motorcycle [we] ever tested." I lived in Cambridge, Massachusetts, and the year was 1969. It was a BSA Lightning, and I got it, slightly used, for $1,400.

I mistrusted the Lightning right from the start, probably because of the yachting flag decals the previous owner had stuck all over the battery cowling. It seemed like something a frat guy might do, and it bothered me, too, that I had no idea what the flags meant.

I bought the bike right after the lovefest at Woodstock, just before an attempted reconciliation with my first wife. My daughter Sara was three years old, my son Kyle was on the way, and I bought the bike in an attempt to hang on to the bit of freedom I had found during our separation, as a hedge against what I'd come to view as the suffocating bourgeois life my wife seemed determined to lead.

The Lightning had a congenital oil leak. I went through two or three different oil pumps, but in the nine months I owned it, I never managed to straighten the problem out. However, apart from the very distracting sensation of hot oil soaking your pant leg, it was a gorgeous machine—a shining, wonderfully throaty motorcyle that was frighteningly fast. True, the bike had problems. But then, so did I, and I became terribly attached to it in the way you only get with things you know can't possibly last.

One afternoon I was whizzing along, heading north out of Harvard Square and into the big winding turn that leads down to the Broadway underpass. It was lovely, an October day, and I was thinking that perhaps a beautiful woman was watching or whatever a young man thinks when he is about to do something fabulously stupid. Then I heeled that bike over, tucked it into the bend, and rolled on the throttle.

Maybe the pavement surface changed, maybe I hit a patch of oil, but instantly I was down and sliding into that tunnel. Sliding on my side, then on my back, then on my other side. It seemed that I might skid like that forever. Just ahead of me, my motorcycle clattered along, trailing a cloud of sparks like some stricken comet. I heard the urgent screech of brakes as motorists swerved to avoid me. In the back of my mind I realized the kind of danger I was in, but the entire span of the accident, the only thing I could think was My bike! My bike! My bike!

My first wife was sophisticated, high-strung, motivated. In short, she was all the things that I was not. By 1969, she had waited a couple of years for me to finish college and get my life together. After a six-month separation, she was disheartened to learn that my idea of getting it together involved buying a motorcycle and choosing a trade.

But working in the trees, as I've done now for twenty-six years, I'd rediscovered my love of the outdoors. And having spent a good part of the '60s trying and failing to please her conservative, hippie-baiting parents, I found my new tree friends irresistible. They were renegades, questers, felons; men who lived at the edge of the law, at the outer limits of gravity. My wife took our new baby home to live with her parents, and filed for divorce. By that spring I had sold the Lightning.

My first ride on an American V-twin is on Chaz's Harley 1000XL Café Racer, a sleek, stylish-looking Sportster with a tiny quarter-faring and stubby "clip-on"–style handlebars designed to configure the rider into a racer's crouch. We actually *are* sitting at a café when Chaz very casually asks me if I want to ride the Sportster home. I'm surprised and thrilled. Surprised because I haven't ridden a bike in over twenty years. Thrilled because it means Chaz must really trust me.

Chaz lights up the Harley for me with a touch of the starter button (what he calls the "electric foot"). He offers a brief orientation to the controls, but I pay little attention. Mostly, I'm preoccupied with the dozen ways I could spaz out and, to the hilarity of noonday onlookers, drop this shiny black crotch rocket right in the middle of the street. I make it away from the curb without incident, through my first corner and my first shift. This is so different from my old Lightning, it seems like another species. It's not so much faster, it's just the *feel* of it, the rhythm. I lope along in second for a couple of blocks, then hit third. I "grab a handful" and the V-twin lunges ahead, seems to gallop, like some fierce winged horse, so that my eyes tear up, the blacktop becomes a blur, and the boulevard trees flick past like shadows in an intoxicating burst of light and air and sound.

There is something about the promise these machines hold out to me. It seems I have endowed them with a great power to change things, or, more to the point, to take me beyond my own limits. I once believed the same thing about climbing trees, and for all I know they are all a part of my composition now, like carbon or calcium or strontium.

One afternoon I'm summoned to Chaz's garage with the photos I took of a pair of Scouts we'd looked at in Portland. Chaz wants to show them to a guy known as "Indian Mike" from Bozeman. On the way over, I understand that, although he hasn't bought these two bikes yet, Chaz is already in the process of peddling one off to finance the other.

Mike is tall and rangy. Like Chaz, he sports a tuft of hair on his underlip and he has a little rattail. He gives me his card and I see that, among other things, he is a photographer and a Motorcycle Safety Instructor. There are old burn scars up and down his arms, and later on Chaz tells me Mike was a roughneck in the Texas oil fields, badly burned in a blowout. He opens his wallet, shows me pictures of his Indians. He tells me about a place in Seattle where you can send your old six-volt Indian generator and they convert it to a twelve-volt for $150.

Then, while Chaz is in the house, I tell Mike about the basketcase Chief I've just bought.

Mike nods his head, tells me wistfully about the 30ci Scout Junior he bought from Chaz a few years back. The heads turned out to be full of water, completely ruined. "By far," Mike says, "it was the worst fucking I ever took in the motorcycle game."

This is the most unsettling conversation I've had. I try to reassure myself with the fact that Mike and Chaz appear to still be friends.

"Oh sure," says Mike. "We're still friends." He grins ruefully. "You know Chaz. He's just so charming, I always keep coming back for more."

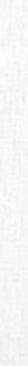

CHAPTER 3

PARTS MOTHERS

THREE DAYS AFTER I BUY THE CHIEF, WE FIND OUT ABOUT THE baby. I think about trying to return it, but in the end, Caroline and I both know it's too late to back out now.

We decide not to go public for a couple of months, but this is a strategy that proves much more difficult for me than it does for her. It seems that nearly every week I've spilled my guts again, sworn yet another unwitting friend to secrecy. It's as if I am compelled to tell other people my news in order to believe it myself.

In much the same way that I have a heightened awareness of V-twin motorcycles, I am suddenly aware of pregnant women. They seem to be everywhere now, at the market, the restaurant, the lumberyard. They are lovely, swelling. Have they been there all along, or do I somehow summon them up?

Sometime toward the end of June, even Caroline can stand it no longer and we both begin to blurt out the news. There is a brief phase where people seem incredulous; at a cocktail party one woman tells me over and over: "You *guys*! You guys are just so *brave*!"

I believe this is meant as a compliment, but still, it's unnerving. It makes it sound less like we're having a baby, more like we're about to swap kidneys.

Chaz's wife Yvonne is the first to swing into action. Yvonne has an impish grin, complemented by the don't-mess-with-me looks of a woman who spent three years bartending at the toughest joint in town. Her hair is cut short at the front and sides. The rest of it foams down her back in a shower of jet-black ringlets. Yvonne's *mother* is my age, fifty-one, and she just came in second in the Missoula Motorcycle Swap Meet wet T-shirt contest.

One evening Yvonne parks the family van in our drive and duck-walks up the back steps with several Hefty bags of maternity clothes slung over her shoulder and a Marlboro in her teeth. She squints against the smoke, whumps the bags down on our couch, dumps them out, and begins to go through them, setting aside the things Caroline thinks she can use. While she's doing this, she tells Caroline the story of delivering her first child, ten years before. A group of Chaz's biker friends in Butte heard the news, promptly suited up, and rode 120 miles west with a rare gift: an infant-size black and orange T-shirt that read "Harley Fuckin' Davidson."

It's not long before the rest of the Sisterhood has discovered us, and for a number of weeks all our women friends with young children show up at our door with boxes and bags of maternity wear: leggings, overalls, maternity bras. Some of them fit better than others, but none of them fit or look better than the bag of clothes Yvonne brought to us.

I'm touched by the generosity of it, this elaborate network of women helping each other out. But I keep wondering, If these two events really *do* somehow run parallel, why is it that there are no men pulling up in front of the house, unloading boxes of Indian parts for me and my Chief?

For the time being at least, I'm content just to observe that the floor beneath our reading lamp has become littered with a whole new literature: *Old Bike Journal, Rocky's Indian Parts,* and *Chrome Specialties* catalogues, along with *Breastfeeding Your Baby* and *Modern Maternity* magazines. There's a book called *What to Expect When You're Expecting* and another titled *Iron Redskin,* and they seem to coexist nicely.

So once again there are motorcycles in my life, and somehow there are once again children. Can I get it right this time, this husband-and-father business? Can I really put this old bike back together? And am I kidding myself to think I can do both?

Late in June I receive a call from my daughter, Sara, who lives in Washington, D.C. I tell her that we are expecting a baby in January and that I'm also rebuilding a motorcycle.

"It sounds like a midlife crisis run amok," one of us quips, though I can't remember if it was her or if it was me.

She's excited to hear our news, but the reason she's really calling is to tell me that her brother, my son Kyle, is in trouble.

My son has been charged with stealing a mountain bike. He seemed as puzzled by his actions as everyone else, and told his big sister he had no idea why he did it. But I think I know why—he did it just to see what would happen.

Because of a bitter feud with my children's stepfather, I didn't see Sara for nearly ten years. I haven't seen Kyle since he was three years old, so when I dream about him he is always a little boy, even though he's just turned twenty-five. Kyle went to school in Colorado and graduated in

'94; I was in the area that spring and I tried to see him, but after much anticipation, many arrangements and phone calls, he gave me the slip. Right now, Kyle is a kind of phantom in my life. He exists only in my dreams. For all I know, that's the way I exist for him. At least for the time being, I know this is the way he prefers it. And when I think about the kind of mess we've all helped to make, I really can't blame him a bit.

I ask Sara if she's worried about her brother, and she falls silent a moment. Then she says, "Yes. I am."

I hang up the phone and call my ex-wife for the first time in a long, long while. She tells me that, as nearly as she can determine, the reason Kyle manages to stay in trouble so much of the time is that he's so much like me. This strikes me as a fairly limited assessment of the situation. But if he is, in fact, just like me, well then his real problem is, at the age of twenty-five, he has no particular skills and has not yet found what he really wants to do. If he is like me, then he has discovered that a perfectly good way to pass the time is to start testing things: His nerve. The people who love him. The Colorado judicial system.

My ex-wife tells me things are not looking good: He's jumped his parole to go back to New York. He didn't bother to tell anybody what he was doing, and so the state of Colorado sent a marshal out after him. The marshal flew back to Colorado with him, and his mom followed them out on the next flight and tried to talk the judge out of a jail sentence. It didn't work. Kyle has some priors, so they put him in a minimum-security outfit for a week.

"And how are you doing with all this?" I ask my ex-wife.

"Oh," she says, *"terrible."*

My son's sentence runs concurrent with a canoe trip a group of us are making down a fifty-mile stretch of the Missouri. The river is broad and mostly smooth, running through the wild and semiarid terrain known as "the Breaks," where the river winds past coulees full of bighorn sheep and mule deer, and huge sandstone cliffs rise hundreds of feet above the water. The trees are in full cotton and it drifts through the air, lighting on the water as we put in at Coalbanks Landing. Everyone cites the beginning of the Fellini movie *Amarcord*. There is much good-natured bitching about the mud and the insects, but we are a merry crew nonetheless. There are ten of us with five canoes, three dogs, and one toddler, and we drift along, watch the nighthawks and eagles slice through the skies, watch the ragged flights of Missouri River pelicans.

Each evening we put in early for cocktails, and about this time we tell stories, spray golf balls through the sagebrush, read aloud from the Lewis and Clark diaries. And in the midst of this expanse of nearly limitless space, I know that somewhere down in Colorado, my phantom son sits in a cell, watching bad television, maybe smoking those crummy jailhouse cigarettes. . . .

I invent several scenarios, such as flying down to see him, flying him back up here to live with us. Getting him a job on the fire crews for the summer. I see him becoming a smoke jumper, something *I* always wanted to do, and he should probably have an Indian, too, so we can ride together. But when all these fantasies disperse, my biggest fear reveals itself—that, if and when I make my long-awaited entrance, I will have nothing very much to offer Kyle.

Shortly after we get off the river, I go to the doctor's with Caroline. The obstetrician puts a Doppler mike to her belly, and for the first time we hear the heartbeat. How *fast* it is, like a hummingbird's, yet how *strong*!

We had thought Caroline was in her thirteenth week, but the doctor tells us it's the fourteenth. Caroline and I gasp. Everything keeps getting moved up. Everything is going faster and faster. The doctor schedules an amniocentesis for late in July, and I make a wisecrack: "Hey, honey. We can still make it to Sturgis!" Even the doctor laughs.

We leave the clinic boggled by it all. This baby is no longer an abstraction. We leave, too, with the conviction that the child is surely a boy, though neither of us can begin to say why.

Three out of three Indian owners I talk to tell me that unless I have the shop, the tools, and the time, I should have my motor restored by a professional.

"It's got to be Ken Edmiston," Chaz says flatly. "He's the only guy to do it."

"Why *him*?" I ask.

"Because not only is he the cheapest, he's also the best. Look," he says, indicating the 45ci motor in little Willa's Mustang scooter. "If he does this kind of work on Willa's motor, think what he can do on yours."

The engine *is* immaculate. The heads and cases are painted aluminum, the bolts are cadmium plated, the valve guides are fresh chrome. If the inside looks anything like the outside, then the man does terrific work. Still, I can't help thinking how infrequent it is that a guy who is the very best at something is also the cheapest.

"How does it run?" I ask.

"I don't know yet," says Chaz. "I haven't gotten around to trying to start it."

In the end, though, I realize I've put myself in Chaz's hands, and if Chaz puts *himself* in Ken's hands, well, then I will too. Still, I can't let go of the idea there is a precarious domino logic to this whole spiritual guide–motorcycle mentor business—if your mentor's a lemon, then everyone else who works on the bike will be bad. But it's way too late to second-guess this now.

As the Portland trip approaches, I'm increasingly reluctant to go without fixing the cooling-fin damage on that front cylinder. Finally Chaz says, "Hey. If those fins are really bothering you, I might have a better jug for you."

I go back home to pull the flawed cylinder. Without a special wrench, I do this with some difficulty, and when I do, the first thing I see is a lot of jagged alloy at the base of the pistons. My heart sinks. Why didn't I take that motor apart before I bought it? (But I know the answer to that: Because I didn't want to go looking for trouble. Because I was feeling lucky that day. Because the motor *spoke* to me.)

Chaz swaps me for a better-looking barrel and tells me that the broken metal I saw by the cylinder boss is what's left of the splash guards, that lots of people chiseled those away with the thought that, this way, more oil would get up to the piston.

"Really, Fred," he says with some amusement, "this kind of thing will be the *least* of your worries."

I pick up Chaz at dawn the next morning. When I walk in, he's packing a valise with boxer shorts, a large revolver, and some Harley parts to deal along the way.

What about the revolver?

"That's in case we run into any unsavory types," he tells me. We flip open the back of my little wagon and toss in a Scout motor, also bound for Ken Edmiston. Under the weight of my Chief motor too, the rear end sags noticeably. I close the lid. Chaz climbs in, pops the seat back, and sleeps all the way to Coeur d'Alene.

Four hours out we stop west of Spokane for a late breakfast. In the course of the conversation Chaz asks, abruptly, if I am a drinker. The question takes me by surprise, but I tell him no. Not particularly, anyway. At least, not the way I *used* to be.

"How about yourself?" I ask. This line of questioning has begun to make me curious.

Chaz shakes his head. "Nope. Not for seven years."

I ask him if he went through AA and he stirs his coffee, tells me no, he didn't, that he couldn't stand that outfit, that they're too sanctimonious.

He falls silent for a moment, then he says, "Yvonne's an addict." His voice is flat, soft. "Seven years ago I told her I'd clean up if she'd clean up."

"So what happened?"

He shrugs his shoulders. "I did and she didn't. Coke, pot—I quit doing everything. I even quit drinking beer. But it hasn't worked out."

He tells me that she's been known to disappear for days. He can never tell when she will take off on a binge, just as he can no longer tell when she's stoned or when she's not.

"No tracks?"

Chaz shakes his head. "She smokes it. Snorts it. Eats it. Hell, she does everything *but* shoot it."

He tells me Yvonne got caught dealing Mexican heroin a few years back and brought the DEA down on them on a Friday afternoon.

"They wanted her source," Chaz says. "We were up against the wall. The whole family. There was a nine-millimeter right up my nose."

He smiles without humor. "It was just like on TV, man. But it seems even the idea of jail won't keep her from using. Once she told me that the times I thought were the best we'd ever had together, those were all when she was stoned."

I can tell that, in a crazy way, that particular statement was harder for him to take than anything the DEA could have laid on him. It's an odd moment. Chaz doesn't seem bitter about it. He doesn't even seem particularly blue. He just seems like a man who needs to get something off his chest. I wished I had something to tell my new friend that might make him feel better. But I don't. We get back in the car and drive on.

Carlton, Oregon, is rural, green, and rolling. There is a mile-long driveway leading to a sprawling ranch house on a hilltop, surrounded by oaks and stout rail fencing. Several late-model vehicles are parked in the drive. After a hard winter in Missoula, the landscape looks soft, fertile, lush as bluegrass country. I've forgotten about the coast, that feeling of ease and prosperity. There's *money* out here. The *Coast*. Good old Beulahland.

Ken comes out to greet us. He was a Marine in World War II, a Team Seattle Indian racer from 1946 to '48, and now he's a genial, youthful-looking seventy-five. I try, but I can't think of a soul in Missoula who makes seventy-five look so good.

His bike collection is spectacular: Chiefs, Scouts, and a couple of Triumphs, impeccably restored. His shop is huge, bright, immaculate, and organized. There are gear-head lathes, arborlaps and truing stands, machining tools of every description. Engine parts are arranged neatly on the walls and in well-marked bins. He shows us several works in progress, like the modified 57ci Scout motor, stroked out so deeply the pistons seem to disappear on the downstroke. We look at several beautifully restored Chief motors waiting for their owners on a steel bench, with little tags and clean shop rags over the intake and exhaust ports, and I think, Oh God, let this be me!

Ken does a quick appraisal of my motor and I hold my breath. What if he says something like "Christ! I can't work on *this*!"

But my fears are quickly put to rest. He points out the fact that my cylinders don't match—the front one Chaz gave me is a square-based military, the rear one is a round-based prewar. We trail along behind him as he goes off to a storage shed, selects a match for the square-based cylinder off a shelf of several dozen, swaps me even across the board. I have a quick flash of the mysterious parts lore, the beneficent old man.

I leave my motor with Ken without even a claim slip, just as you would at your friendly neighborhood shade-tree mechanic's. I leave it there like that because Chaz says it's OK.

I'm relieved to get out of there. It's understandable how Ken can be the best *and* the cheapest. Plainly, money is not a problem in his life, and the Indian motor rebuilding business seems more a hobby. But the softness and verdure of that coastal landscape makes the Montana winter we just went through seem particularly dreary, shriveling. The sheer opulence of Ken's shop and layout makes Chaz's place—and, for that matter, my own—seem impoverished and desperate.

All the way home, Chaz rails about Bootsy. To this point, Chaz's remarks about him have been circumspect, but it turns out that Bootsy is Chaz's archrival in the Missoula vintage motorcycle game. Chaz sees little difference between Bootsy and the rapacious Autralians who scour the countryside for every last vintage machine and part. I listen intently. This is the first time I've heard Chaz on a rant.

We stop in Coeur d'Alene at Lucky's Harley shop to say hello and chat. We walk around the shop for a few minutes. Chaz tries to interest Lucky in a Harley frame he has back in Missoula. Lucky seems wary. Then Lucky tries to sell Chaz a BSA transmission and rear wheel. Chaz turns up his nose.

It's well past midnight when we arrive back in Missoula. I drop Chaz off at his North Side garage. The skies are overcast with low, rain-laden clouds, and I notice there are large puddles along the curbs and many heavy tree limbs down.

"That must have been a hell of a storm," I say as we pull up to his shop.

Chaz collects his gear and says nothing. I realize Chaz isn't much concerned about the size of the rain puddles or the big downed limbs, either. What Chaz is concerned about as we arrive back home from two days on the road is the fact that his van is gone and, most likely, so is Yvonne.

CHAPTER 4

MERLIN AND MAGOO

RIGHT FROM THE START, I KNOW I'LL GO TO MAGOO FOR MY paint and bodywork. I know this because Chaz will have it no other way. In the course of my first visit, I begin to understand that Chaz's estimates for my project costs are, well, estimates. Chaz told me rebuilding my tanks would run "from three to five hundred," but on my first visit to his shop, Magoo tells me he won't take on the job for any less than $700.

I look down at Magoo's watchdog, an unbecoming Rottweiler cross named Merlin. Merlin watches me closely, shows some teeth. Merlin is onto me. It's clear he's marked me for some kind of fraud, and he's going to be tough to disabuse of this notion.

"*Seven hundred* bucks?" I tell Magoo. "Hell, I can go buy brand-new aftermarket welded [as opposed to soldered] reproductions for the same price. Then I could turn around and sell the ones I have for four hundred dollars and have an overall expenditure of only three hundred or so."

This is my best shot, but when I'm done explaining this Magoo simply nods his head.

"Sure," he says, reasonably. "You could do that. In fact, you'd probably be crazy *not* to."

Was it possible that I'd gained some ground?

"So. Can you cut me a little slack on that price, then?"

Magoo shakes his head. He is politely adamant. It seems as if a couple minutes passes before he finally says, "I'll tell you what, though. I'll guarantee it won't be any *more* than seven hundred bucks."

This is my first price skirmish. Since there are no fenders included with my basketcase, I will probably have to buy reproductions, which means the tanks will be the only original sheet metal on the bike. Why this seems so important I can't quite say. It just is, and it seems to be $300 worth of importance. I console myself with the fact that not only do I keep the original parts this way, I also keep the money in town with a local artisan.

Magoo tells me that between the silver solder spatter and the toxicity of the flux, rebuilding Indian tanks is a particularly thankless, not very cost-efficient task. While I'm still thinking about the reproductions (the "repops"), Magoo shows me another pair of Chief tanks he's restored, sitting on a drying rack. They are gorgeous, perfect teardrop shapes in an apple-green primer, and they look *wonderful.* I feel myself crumble. I hand over my own phlegmy-looking tanks, tell Magoo to have at them. As I leave his garage, I file it away in the back of my mind that so far Chaz's estimates of what things will cost are off by about a hundred percent.

A month later I'm back—with my frame fully stripped and ready for the shop. Magoo's place is just over the mountain four miles to the east, and past midsummer, the yards are full of towering sunflowers, colossal cornstalks, canoes and rafts up on sawhorses. There are no curbs in East Missoula, and log trucks and heavy machinery are parked tight on the houses like great, dust-covered oxen.

Magoo's shop is clean, organized, well-lighted. There are welder's tanks, jigs, vises, presses, anvils, and an airtight paint room around the corner with a huge exhaust fan.

Inside, the paint-room door is decorated with doodles, which include a school of porpoises, a laughing lightbulb, and a peculiar-looking series of bubbles. Inside the spray room is a mysterious logo—flywheels and pistons over a buffalo skull—and in ghostly lettering, just visible beneath the overspray, it says "PARTS FATHER."

There is someone else's Chief frame in the work space, and I feel a twinge of jealousy, probably because, with its shining black paint and fresh plunger spring covers, it's much farther along than mine is.

Magoo is slight, wiry, in his forties. He has a thoughtful air, a salt-and-pepper beard, and he looks more like a professor of anthropology than a biker. Like Chaz, he wears rimless spectacles; like Chaz, he wears his hair in a long ponytail and he's from the eastern part of the state. A quick tour of his garage reveals a beautifully restored '55 Panhead Harley and a '48 Chief still in primer. Parts Father rebuilt the engine for it, back in 1990.

Magoo and Chaz have been running buddies for twenty years, but while I've come to know Chaz as a wisecracker and deadpan artist, Magoo is low-key, almost unnervingly quiet, and I spend my first visits with him vaguely uncomfortable.

Magoo helps me unstrap my Chief frame from the back of my truck, and together we carry it inside, where I meet a great hulking biker named Kevin, who sits drinking his way through a six-pack of Löwenbräu dark.

Then I bring in the little box of American Heritage panhead

tappets that Chaz sent along, and Magoo seems pleased. I can't tell if I've curried favor or not, but Magoo seems friendly, in spite of our price skirmish the other day. We squat on the concrete, have a look at my frame. He points out the places where the front loop has been abraded by the crashbar mounts. Then he points out the goose-egged rear-engine mounting hole, which could indicate things weren't fitting quite right. He tells me that the Indian frame is about the heaviest there is, and that, at least so far, mine looks to be pretty straight.

Magoo's girlfriend, Karen, comes out to join us. She is cheerful, pretty, a wisecracker. She rides a 750 BMW and has a stained-glass business of her own. Karen studies my frame for a moment, then grins. "Wow," she says. "You got a *lot* of work ahead of you, don't you?"

In August, I find myself up a very large tree, a two-hundred-year-old, ninety-foot-tall, beetle-killed ponderosa pine, right on the shore of Swan Lake. I've worked my way up two-thirds of it when the afternoon wind kicks in and the tree begins to pitch and sway, the way a conifer will do when you've cut off the better part of its branches.

This is a very expensive job, and just below me, there's lots of high-priced carpentry to damage if I get a little frisky. In fact, there's no small amount of tension surrounding this situation. I'm working this tree with my good friend Neil on the ropes. On the ground with Neil is a combination security guard and maintenance man. He seems nice enough, the maintenance man, but he is so nervous, I can barely stand to look at him. Every twenty minutes or so he whips out a cellular phone to report to the owner, some out-of-state corporate bigwig, on the progress of the job. It's starting to drive me crazy.

I look above me, to the ragged dried-up stub where the original top blew off years ago. There is a right-angle crook in the trunk, where the tree has formed a new top from a lateral branch, and it goes up another twenty-five feet.

This is where I have to go next. It *looks* sound enough, but talking myself up these tops is always a nerve-racking thing. Quitting the job, quitting the business once and for all, has become a kind of siren song, but finally I whinge and sigh, mutter the usual apologies to everyone I've wronged, backstabbed, and cheap-shot. Then I think of what the Lakota used to say: "It's a good day to fight. It's a good day to die."

There's not a reason in the world why this incantation should work for a white man, yet it never fails to quiet my mind. So at last I unclip my short line and free-climb the last twenty feet into the top of the pine.

To the east, the Swan Mountains rise 10,000 feet, while to the west, a great sweep of forest sprawls off to the edge of the horizon. I can never look at this arboreal continuum and not think of how, before the Europeans arrived, it was possible for a squirrel to climb a tree in Maryland and work his way from treetop to treetop, all way to the Mississippi.

This is not unlike the way I came west. For years I climbed trees all over the country—Maine, New Hampshire, Vermont, Massachusetts, Connecticut, New York, both the Carolinas, and Virginia. I moved to Boulder in 1977 and climbed trees there until I wound up in Missoula a year or so later, and when I went to graduate school at the University of Montana, I climbed more trees to support myself.

I finished my master's degree and climbed more trees. Eventually I wrote my way into Stanford University in 1988, where for three years I taught a series of fiction workshops for undergraduates, many of whom were a good deal smarter than I. Every day I rode my ten-speed across the quad with a knapsack full of student work. Every day I wore clean Levi's with no oil or pine pitch on them. I attended countless readings, lectures, and colloquiums, and afterward I went to the faculty lounge, where I drank chardonnay with Brian Moore, sherry with Doris Lessing, Anchor Steam with Robert Stone, and put it all on the department tab. There was interest in my novel, and it appeared a teaching job would follow. My last five months at Stanford, all I did was hold my breath, wait for my next break. So when my lectureship ran out, the book didn't sell, and my job prospects evaporated, I took it hard. We packed our belongings and returned to Montana, where I'd swear that, seven years later, I'm right back where I started.

Gingerly I climb into the tip-top of the old ponderosa. I throw my short line around the trunk, but before I can even clip in, I'm startled nearly out of my wits. Right there in front of me are somebody's carved initials. It's hard to explain, but I wouldn't be more surprised if I'd actually found a *person* there, waiting for me. I study the initials a moment: "N.W." Nathanael West. Norbert Wiener. Was it some kid? The W is partly covered with tree callus, so it was a good while ago. Judging by the depth and precision of the carving, whoever did it was comfortable enough up there to take a good long time with it.

Who *was* this person who ascended this great tree on this tiny island in the middle of Montana, just to carve his initials at the top? It strikes me I may have found the equivalent of my loose change, ZagNut bar, and toy jeep in a mason jar, buried long ago on a hillside, underneath a hickory tree.

I finish topping the old pine out, leave a fifty-foot standing butt, descend on my rope, and prepare to fell it. The hard part is over for me now, but it always seems to be the point where everyone else gets nervous. It's a little tight—the chalet that's under construction is on one side and there's a boathouse on the other, but it looks like a clear shot down the middle and I'm cocky now, like I'm really in control. An armed security guard has joined us for the final cut, and before I light up the big felling saw, I'm so confident I grin and say, "Hey, you guys. If I fuck this up, will you give me a ten-minute head start?"

Nobody laughs. In fact, nobody says anything for quite a while. Finally the armed security man turns to me and with great sincerity says, "Tell you what, bub. You fuck this up, we'll probably be running right alongside you."

Because of his hauling business, his broad assortment of machinery, and his ranch-boy ingenuity, I've invited Chaz to throw in with my tree business. I do all the climbing and pruning, then Chaz does the cleanup and brush hauling. This arrangement means we get to trade off guru-izing on bikes and trees, and mostly we do all right with this arrangement, though it *is* an awful lot of time together. One day I'm hanging around the Carnal Garage and he suddenly tells me he has a present for me.

"Really?" I say. "What for?"

"It's about time I did you a good turn," he says. He repairs to an anteroom, comes back with a small box.

"Wow," I say and give it a shake. "Is it a magneto?"

"No."

"A shift-linkage bell crank?"

"No."

I open the box and I'm startled: It is a very handsome reproduction of the famous war-bonnet chief front fender light, a chromium base, with an Indian face lens that lights up.

I go home delighted, but still unsure of what it means that Chaz might feel like I'm "due for a good turn."

I get home, open up the box, and show Caroline.

"Cool," she says. "Where'd you get *that*?"

"Chaz gave it to me," I tell her.

"So," says Caroline, "does this mean you guys are going steady?"

For the first time in her pregnancy, Caroline is nervous. Dr. Richards is reassuring, puts her on the examining table, hooks her belly to the ultrasound machine, hits the lights, and the next thing I know, I'm watching our child, this little miniature being. I take quick inventory: Two arms and two legs. Hands and feet all there. My God, is it ever *active,* bouncing, treading water like it's in a hot tub, then doing something that looks quite a lot like a flip turn off the uterine wall.

They call this amniocentesis procedure "the stick." It begins to get scary. The doctor unwraps a syringe of veterinarian proportions, watches the monitor, prepares to insert it, and I keep wanting to holler out, "Look out! Stay *down,* little baby!"

It all goes smoothly, though we won't have the result for another ten days. The nurse's name is Patty.

"First baby?" says Patty.

Technically that's not the case, but we both nod and smile. Patty tells us we should try to really *savor* the next six months, to be sure to sleep in whenever we can. She tells us that, what's more, "from about January tenth on, your mealtimes will never be the same again."

Two days later Yvonne delivers an eight-pound, seven-ounce boy, whom they call Baby Aydyn.

One week later we discover we're having a little girl.

CHAPTER 5

THE 12-MILLION-HORSEPOWER PARTY

THEY COME UP FAST FROM BEHIND, IN PAIRS OR FLIGHTS OF three, four, and five, their headlights bobbing, flickering in the waves of heat. They are bare-shouldered, burned dark by the sun, and as they heave alongside to pass, they go from the spectral to the suddenly substantial, like so many beer-bellied wraiths. Arrayed in a grab bag of sociopathic accoutrements (the best of the huns, brigands, gypsies, buccaneers), they're all bound for Sturgis, just like me.

On their heads they wear bandannas, scarves, or, occasionally, a snug-fitting pillbox number—something like a cross between a yarmulke and a welder's hat. They ride Harleys, most of them the newer Evolution models, with the occasional Shovelhead or Panhead among them. I'm proud of my newfound ability to tell one from the other, though Chaz can tell them apart by sound alone.

Every twentieth bike or so is foreign: a Honda Gold Wing, some ersatz Harley of Japanese origin, or a blocky-looking BMW, known within the biker circle as "Flying Bricks." Whatever the nationality, you can generally tell the imports from a mile away. *Their* riders are the ones in the helmets.

It's a crazy time of year, mid-August. Our small-town streets are sweltering, snarled with last-gasp vacation traffic. It's the advent of fall, but not quite. The tail end of summer, but something more. It's a crack between the seasons, a time of passage. A time for all the sad and too-familiar pre-autumn rituals, such as those tentative and lugubrious pre-season football broadcasts, those first back-to-school sales. Or, our local specialty, the elk-calling clinics, where scores of student buglers create a sound as mournful and bizarre as you'll ever hear, a noise that spirals up from the sporting-goods parking lots like Al Green choking on a hairball. It seems we've reached that point when summer has gone on way too long.

Originally, the plan calls for me to drive to Sturgis with Chaz, but he has wisely chosen to stay home with Yvonne. As I drive along, I'm thinking that it's funny—this time last year, I probably would have driven six hundred miles to stay *away* from the Annual Black Hills Motorcycle Rally, the "heartbeat of the biker nation."

Of course, that was all before the Chief.

In Bozeman it's 103 degrees. To the north, the Bridger Range bakes and shimmers in the sun as I follow the interstate east along the Yellowstone, near the old trail the settlers once called "the Bloody Bozeman." By the time I roll through Billings and angle south, through Little Bighorn country, it has reached 110 degrees. My pickup has no air-conditioning, and I find it makes little difference if I leave the windows up or down. The heat has induced a kind of a hypnotic state. I've borrowed a friend's country-and-western tapes to play, and by now a Garth Brooks song called "Friends in Low Places" is lodged in my brain like a tick.

An hour south of Billings, I choose to stay on the interstate and not take the Lodge Grass shortcut to the Black Hills. I do this thinking that, this way, I will be more likely to find a motel room for the night. It is the first of many midlife-driven decisions I will make in the course of this trip, decisions that will awaken in some part of me that vague sense of scorn I now reserve for the helmeted import riders. It is the kind of scorn that makes me think: A *motel* room on a run to Sturgis? I should drive on past midnight and sleep in the dirt.

By the time I get to Sheridan it's cooled off to 103. I get the last vacancy, crank up the air-conditioning, switch on the tube. It's the first Monday-night game of the preseason. The matchup is a pair of Rust Belt teams, and the game is so half-assed that even the colorman seems embarrassed. I find another channel, and it's World War II. Somewhere on any TV in any motel room in the country, it's *always* World War II. Now a couple of scholars are arguing about Hiroshima. Was the bomb *necessary*? I switch the TV off. I've been watching this war as long as I can remember now, which is nearly fifty years. World War II is so familiar to me, it's actually comforting.

Outside my room, a Harley pulls in, idles briefly, then shuts down. I guess that it's an Evo by its brassy exhaust note, and in a few minutes I step outside to see if I'm right. As it turns out, it's a Shovelhead, and a sunburned rider in a welder's yarmulke sits astride it a couple rooms away. He tells a motel patron about a biker he saw eat it, sideswiped while riding through Yellowstone Park. The Shovelhead rider spits, shakes his head, says "Life is cheap," then pops down his kickstand. I return to my room, turn the TV back to World War II.

The next morning I gas up in Gillette and meet a westbound biker, still in morning leathers, coming out of the Mini Mart with a doughnut and coffee. I hold the door open for him, ask how Sturgis was, and he grins, chomps his doughnut, and jelly spurts everywhere. He swears cheerfully and says, "It's about like last year. Crowded."

"Any campsites left?"

"Sure," he says. "I mean, there usually are. People come and go all the time." He finishes his doughnut, wipes the jelly off his leathers. "But I wouldn't spend the night in that nuthouse for a million bucks."

It makes me think about what Chaz says, which is: "The younger you are, the more you're going to like Sturgis."

The Black Hills are situated near the exact geographic center of the United States, in the northwest corner of South Dakota. A Lakota woman once showed me a satellite photo of the Great Plains and pointed out that from outer space, the Black Hills appear as a great, dark mass in the shape of a heart.

The Sioux considered the Black Hills one of the great power centers of this country. It's possible to think that when white men finally uprooted the Black Hills' mysteries and dug up the gold, it was like opening Pandora's box. Here, in this epicenter of Indian spirituality, the acres of open pit mines, the arrogance of Mount Rushmore, the idiocy of "The Flintstones' Bedrock City" are all the evidence you'd ever need that pernicious and chaotic spirits are now at large in this world.

My first inkling of the scale of the rally is when I pass the Deadwood Pancake House and see a lot full of Harleys, a hundred bikes deep.

At Sturgis, you understand immediately how out of it you are, driving a car. You understand it doesn't matter what kind of bike you've got back home in the garage. You've shown up at the most celebrated motorcycle event in the world and you're the guy on four wheels. You're Out of It in a way perhaps you've never been before.

There are traffic jockeys everywhere in their Day-Glo and shorts, gamely trying to regulate the motorcycle flow. The scent of Castrol hangs in the air as the great bikes rev up, rap out, crackle back down to an idle. They swell and fade, swell again till the very pavement seems to vibrate. Bikes shoot off in unexpected directions and the street seems volatile, maybe even fissionable. I am filled with an excitement tinged with dread for something that either is about to happen or could be about to happen, I don't know which.

This year's turnout was around 215,000, but for the sake of convenience, let's round it down to 200,000—that's twice the size of a Super Bowl crowd, in a town of five thousand. Then let's say that most of these people are mounted on Harleys, and that most of the Harleys pump out sixty horsepower and up. You wind up with something in the neighborhood of 12 million horsepower, prowling, growling, roaming the streets.

The Indian Rally is set apart from this pandemonium. It is across town, next to a baseball diamond known as Strong Field. By the time I crawl through the two miles of Harley traffic, it is in full progress.

There is a line of perhaps forty bikes in the infield, shining in the brilliant prairie sunlight. Mostly Chiefs, they are painted in the Indian primary spectrum: blue, yellow, red, black, and white. With their obsolete handshifts and heavy valenced fenders, there is an innocent, toylike quality about these bikes that is almost touching.

Tricked out with enough studs, fringe, and frippery to belong in a Hopalong Cassidy movie, the postwar Indian Chiefs are a wonderful blend of the preposterous and the fabulous. They are machines straight out of a young boy's dreams: equal parts cow pony, fire-breathing dragon, and mechanical wizardry. These machines, as it happens, are the very incarnation of every childhood fantasy of speed, power, and flight I ever had.

Compared to the scene back in town, the Indian Rally is small, even folksy. The crowd looks different: Not so hard-core. Not so standardized. They tend to look as if they do other things besides ride motorcycles. There is an elfin German freelance photographer, his hair dyed black as crankcase oil, shooting the old bikes as fast as he can with a big SpeedGraphic camera. There is a very purposeful-looking reporter from the Sioux Falls *Times* and there is a group of Euro-bikers in vests, cowboy hats, and sandals who stand off by themselves and rubberneck the bikes. I talk to a lanky fellow whose bedroll is lashed to a white Chief with Montana plates. He says he's from Seattle, actually, but he's also from Montana. He says his Chief is a '47, a '46, and a '48, that he restored it ten years ago or maybe it was twelve, that he's been riding it ever since. He talks faster than any human being I've ever met.

There's a shaky old man in a white-billed cyclist's cap and a denim vest, covered with Rally pins. He has a red '47 Chief that just took first prize. I hear he's had his bike for forty years, but I can't get through the crush of people to talk to him. I end up talking instead to a Harley rider from Sioux Falls who's stopped by for a quick look. He has a freshly shaved head with a rattail garnish. I ask him, "What *is* it about Indians?"

"I don't know," he says. "But you come to a place like this here, where you got a thousand bikes rolling by every hour, and nobody even bothers to look. Then all of a sudden, here comes an Indian. Everybody stops and stares, and it's like 'Wow, a *real* motorcycle . . .'"

I recognize Dave Warhank, whose hopped-up '39 Chief was featured in *Indian Illustrated* magazine a month or two back. I know he's from Montana, and I go ovezr to talk. He's thickset, with a Mephisto goatee gone to salt and pepper. He's there with his partner and co-restorer, Tom Benson, whose side-hack Chief was featured in *Old Bike Journal.*

For a while the three of us stand and watch the rally events. There is a kick-start contest, to see how many times you can start and kill your Indian in a minute. This is followed by an event called the Plank Race, to see who can cycle the farthest on a series of two-by-sixes without wobbling off. After that, there's an event involving water balloons and things start to get a little goofy, although it's still fun to watch the old bikes run.

The MC is a heavyset man with a cordless mike.

I recognize him from a video I saw called *Indian Summer,* and I turn to Warhank. "Say, isn't that Hank Beckwith, world-famous restorer of Indians?"

Warhank scowls and shakes his head. "No," he says. "It's not. That's actually Hank 'Dipshit' Beckwith." He spits between his boots.

His partner nods. "Hank 'Dipshit-Fuckhead' Beckwith is who it is. Hey, Dave?" he says to his friend. "Why don't you come help me shove that microphone right up Hank's ass?"

Eventually my new friends become engaged in a conversation about nipple piercing, and I excuse myself, head off to the grandstands for a polish and a Coke. There is a vintage Indian flat-track racer turning slow laps around the oval, raising a cloud of dust. The wind picks up out of the west and people squint, cover their eyes. Hats sail off, tumble across the field. A bride and groom thunder past on a coal-black Sportster, and under the stands I see a biker with his head thrown back, someone's knee in his spine. For a second it's like I'm witness to a mugging, but then I realize the person administering the knee is actually steadying himself while he rebraids his friend's hair.

I called Hank Beckwith myself when I was first considering this project. When I told him what my budget was, he was dismissive, even contemptuous, and inside of five minutes I was given to understand that, unless I was nailing down $100,000 a year, I would be insane to undertake this particular project. I was also given to understand that pretty much anyone I got to work on the motor who wasn't Hank would be bound to screw it up—and screw it up badly. And when I told him that I was thinking of writing a book about it, he allowed there was certainly somebody out there who could do a better book, and that it would probably be out a lot sooner, too.

Restorers like this (of whom there are more than a few) seem bent on making a high-end business out of a craft that has long been the domain of the workingman, a labor of love that, for decades, took place in chilly garages all over the country.

Talking to Beckwith left a bad taste in my mouth, and I hung up the phone thinking, I've just been snobbed by a high-end grease monkey! Beckwith made me want a bumper sticker just like the one Chaz has on the back of his van. The one that says "Die, Yuppie Biker Scum!"

Out in front of the fairgrounds, I walk past a three-quarter-ton flatbed with Alaska license plates. The truck has a ratted-out backcountry look: no front grille, starred-up windshield, stove-in doors. In the back are several mounted spare tires, gas cans, and a familiar-looking pile of junk that turns out to be the better part of a basket-case Chief. A tiny bearded man with shoulder-length hair sits cross-legged on the decking like a tailor as he snips an oil pump gasket from a sheet of cork. It seems he's brought his Indian restoration project on the road with him, just as other people would bring along their needlework or a good book. He's down here from somewhere on the Kenai Peninsula, and while he works, he grouses cheerfully about the delays he's encountered on his 2,200-mile trip. One of these delays is a third-degree burn he suffered along his right arm. "Yeah," he says. "I damn near *cremated* myself. The hose blew off my pressure washer. I spent three days in the hospital before I could get back on the road. That's why I'm running so late."

I can't tell if he means late with his Indian project or late arriving to Sturgis. More than anything I want to tell this guy, who has driven down the Alcan to work on his Indian in the company of other enthusiasts, that Hank Beckwith would think he was wasting his time. Mostly I want to tell him that so I can hear him say "Who the fuck is Hank Beckwith?"

Back in town, Junction Avenue is transformed into a biker's Casbah. In front of the coffee shops, markets, and mom-and-pop drugstores, a hundred tents are pitched and booths are erected. Flags and banners with brand names like Metzeler, Super-Trapp, and Dunlop snap and furl in the prairie wind like pennants from exotic nation-states. The booths along the avenue hawk every kind of motorcycle part and accessory known to man—custom shocks, custom spokes, custom wheels. King and queen seats, sheepskin seat covers, high-rise handlebars. Custom tanks, fenders, pipes, and frames. It seems incredible there could be so much stuff available for what is, essentially, such a simple machine.

I've changed into my black Indian T-shirt in an attempt to enter into the spirit of the thing, though by this time it's clear that nobody much gives a damn if you're in a tux or a clown suit. The only way you're going to enter into the spirit at Sturgis is if you arrive on a large, American-made motorcycle. And even this is subject to controversy; I see T-shirts that state:

.5 Miles and 15,000 dollars
does NOT make you a biker!

This refers to the phenomenon of the biker wanna-be who shells out fifteen grand for a new Evo, then trailers it a thousand miles so he can get dressed up in his outfit and ride it up and down Lazelle Street.

Another shirt I saw a lot of was:

Jane Fonda, American Traitor Bitch!

If the Harley crowd likes their bikes simple and uncomplicated, then it seems to follow that this is the way they like their politics, too. As nearly as I can tell, these are politics that involve a good deal of nostalgia—for a time when we'd never lost a war, when ecology was not such an issue, when gasoline was cheap. A time when Made in the USA meant Best in the World.

Lazelle Street is lined with bikes for as far as you can see. Ranks of Harleys are parked along both curbs, and there is a double row of them down the centerline, too, leaving narrow corridors for the cyclists. Like picadors, the traffic jocks step in and out, work the thundering loop of bikers that flows up one side of Lazelle and then back down the other. The sidewalk is packed with rubberneckers, and the riders are raucous, joyous, on parade. They are mostly men, but there are a number of women on their own Harleys, everything from Sportsters to Wide Glides. The big bikes growl and snort, start quick and stop short, and in the midst of all the noise, smoke, and horsepower, men ripple their pecs, and some of the women smile and bare their chests.

In the parking lot of the Jack Pine Gypsies VFW Hall, I finally see my first cop. He sits grimly in his black-and-white, avoiding eye contact. He is one of the unhappiest-looking men I've ever seen. Inside the hall there's a whole wall dedicated to the history of this event, which was started by the Jack Pine Gypsies in 1940. There's a big wall map stuck with visitors' home-state pins, and there are a couple of women with high plains permanents, smoking cigarettes as they stand by their sewing machines, ready to mend any riven leathers or blown-out Levi's.

There's a large message board, too, with a lone note that reads:

Jerry—Andrea and I are waiting for you back at the bike. Dad.

I walk into a tattoo parlor set up in a Quick Lube garage. A dozen artists buzz away feverishly while customers queue up in the street, waiting to get arms, buttocks, chests, and crotches supercharged with angels, demons, bluebirds, flames, whatever. Ready to do business, some customers have already taken their shirts off. Still others stand patiently with their pants around their ankles, as if awaiting some kind of open-air physical. I wonder how much tequila it would take to make me drop my pants in the middle of downtown Sturgis, while I stand and wait to get a pair of dice inked indelibly onto my genitals. I decide it would take a whole hell of a lot.

On a whim, I flip through a tattoo design book, under the section titled "Indians." I'm looking for the famous war-bonnet chief's head, the Indian trademark throughout the '30s. But all I can find are dusky Sioux maidens with waist-length hair, washboard abdominals, and breasts like footballs.

Rivaling the lines at the tattoo parlors is the one at the entrance of the Black Hills AA Center. But *nobody* is doing the kind of land-rush business of the huge Harley-Davidson shop. More for the clothing aficionado than the motorhead, the aisles are packed with shoppers, all carrying plastic boutique-style HD shopping bags filled with Harley-Davidson chokers, vests, earrings, jeans, all of them priced up with and beyond Ralph Lauren. Perhaps very soon there will be a full line of

Harley-Davidson cosmetics, featuring colognes with names like Shovelhead and Fat Bob-WideGlide. The place seems so pricey that for a moment I can't swear I'm *not* in a Ralph Lauren boutique, except for the three-hundred-pound Hispanic bouncer sitting by the door with a nightstick and a large can of Mace.

It's five o'clock, and I don't yet have a place to pitch my tent. I can see a couple of campgrounds from the road, and they appear stark, shadeless, crowded. I know I'm thinking like a midlife guy, but I cannot make the prospect of a night here sound inviting. I imagine the thunder of Evos, the yowl of rutting bikers, the pitter-patter of urine on my tent fly. I creep along for twenty minutes, stop for a light and ride my clutch. Just ahead is a woman on the back of a Sportster, and she stands out from the crowd. She wears little black boots, sheer stockings, and what looks like a black velvet cocktail dress. All that's really missing is a string of pearls. While they're stopped, she wraps her arms around the driver (in biker argot, her "set of nuts"), nuzzles his neck, and licks his big helmetless ears till they glow cherry red. She runs her hands over his chest and belly, plays him like some large stringed instrument till the light changes and the two of them are off like a shot. It makes me want to say something that sounds very much like a father, something like: "If you're out there listening, baby girl, don't you ever let me catch you on the back of a hog."

The next day, August 9, is the fiftieth anniversary of the bombing of Nagasaki. It's grown cold. The northbound riders pass me in full leathers, sheepskin vests. The seasons have shifted, and overnight we've moved on into fall. Things have changed. I can feel it.

I hear over the radio that in the early morning Jerry Garcia passed away. Jerry was only a year older than me. He will be followed in a matter of days by Mickey Mantle. Things have changed, all right. It's the old August Morbidity. My own introduction to this phenomenon came long ago, August 1973, when a good friend got tangled in his own climbing line and snapped his neck in a roped fall. He was only twenty-four, loved by everyone who knew him. It took me years to get over it. Maybe I never did, as every year about this time I still get a terrible whiff of mortality, a kind of stomach-wrenching fear for the safety of my family and everyone I've ever cared for.

The night I get back from Sturgis I hear about the tornado. They are rare in the mountains. This one happened the day I left for the Black Hills, when an eddy of cold northern air blew down into that heat wave to create a microburst, a confluence of forces violent enough to uproot old growth tamaracks, splinter acres of forest, and wreak havoc around my in-laws' cabin. There are a number of larches left standing, but everything else is blown down or snapped off at about eight feet, the logs jackstrawed every which way. It's incredible that this place—for years the most peaceful and secluded spot I know—could now look like Ground Zero.

I call Ken Edmiston.

He answers the phone: "Yeah?"

I identify myself and ask for the prognosis on my 1941 motor.

"Sure," he says. "Hang on." There is some rustling around on the other end, then he clears his throat, hauls off and gives me a list of a dozen or so parts missing from the guts of my engine, mostly stuff from the primary drive: countershaft sprocket, motor sprocket, front chain, generator drive sprocket, etc. He says that unless I can come up with some of these parts, it will be about $400 more than he originally thought.

For the first time, I begin to get an inkling of how the whole basket-case deal works, which is like a classic bait and switch; the motor changes hands, dealer to dealer, and in the process parts are skimmed, and the rest is sold as "near complete." Or maybe good parts are replaced with crummy ones, if you're that kind of guy.

I go back to my garage and burn a braid of sweetgrass, as the Blackfeet do in their religious ceremonies. I don't even know why. To purify my garage? Sure. Why not? With my tanks and frame in East Missoula and my motor still in Oregon, it looks pretty empty in there.

I switch on the Saturday-night reggae show and turn my attention to the wheels, which, along with the front forks, are about all I have left of the Chief right now. I pop the front wheel—the rusty one—clear of the front fork with a broom handle and start sanding it down with some 220 grit. It cleans up nicely.

While I sand, I think about that odd knife-maker guy my friend Frankie and I ran into in the Union Club bar the other night. Rick, that was his name. First he got Frankie and me to go in on a pitcher of ale with him. We didn't particularly want a pitcher, but we bought it just to shut him up. Then he proceeded to show us his wares—some decent-looking lock-back knives of his own making. The cases were made of buffalo horn and melted-down shell casings. Not a bad deal for $20—if you really like knives. We didn't bite, but Rick kept dropping his price, wouldn't rest till Frankie bought one, and then, finally, till *I* bought one, too. It seemed he'd sold us everything he could, so he started talking metaphysics. Something about how we are all, essentially, spiritual beings. How our time on earth is a kind of chrysalis state. It nearly drove me mad. Frankie must have felt the same, because halfway through the pitcher of ale we didn't want, we packed up the knives we didn't really want either, stood up in the middle of the sermon we weren't that interested in, and hustled our way out of the Union Club before Rick could get to the heart of it all.

CHAPTER 6

HOPPING IT UP

A '47 Indian Chief weighs six hundred pounds. In stock configuration, the motor delivers around forty horsepower, not a whole lot by today's standards. Since I weigh over two hundred pounds and live in the mountains too, I want my Chief to climb those grades without breathing hard. I need to decide if I want to lengthen the Chief's stroke and enlarge the displacement from 74 to 80 cubic inches.

Ken tells me he can do this easily and at no additional cost, if I can come up with a set of 80-inch flywheels. How much will it increase performance? Ken says maybe 10, maybe 15 percent. In the '40s, this was a popular modification among hot-rodders. In the '50s, it was a modification the Indian factory performed itself in an eleventh-hour attempt to recapture their share of the V-twin market.

I didn't realize it till now, but I don't *want* a mellow old bike. I liked the enthusiasm Ken displayed for this particular option, and I tell Chaz I've decided to stroke it.

"Now you're talking!" he says. And at this point, he begins to call me "Stroker," a name Caroline despises, but a name I could really get used to, if it weren't for the ironic backspin Chaz puts on it.

Now I have to locate the parts. First I try to go with factory Indian 80-inchers, but since they were made only from 1951 to '53, they are exceedingly rare, and after calls to a half-dozen parts outfits, nobody can come up with a set. Nobody can even remember the last time they *saw* a set.

If I were conducting my restoration at a more leisurely pace, I would start hitting all the swap meets. But I'm trying hard to ride it next summer, and the likelihood of my bumping into a pair of them at all, especially for much less than $400, are slim to none, so in the interest of pushing ahead I go with a set made by S&S, a famous manufacturer of Harley performance equipment. I rush down to the post office, send off a money order, and have the flywheels shipped directly to Ken. It's amazing how many of these parts outfits operate on a cash-only basis.

In a week's time, I begin to have doubts. By beefing up the flywheels and not upgrading to heavier connecting rods, I may have gone only halfway with this hop-up. Even though Ken has assured me the 74ci rods are fine, I have convinced myself that by using them I have created a weak link in the Chief, a kind of accident waiting to happen. Now I begin to shop around for factory 80ci rods, but as with the flywheels, the originals cannot be found. Again, I have to go to reproductions, and these are $500, made by an outfit called Carillo.

"Carillos? Those are beautiful rods, man," bikers tell me. "*Beautiful.*"

Maybe I don't know a lot about engines. But I know one thing, and that is, the Chief has *got* to have beautiful rods. In short order, I'm back on the phone to Ken, telling him to hold up on the work.

"That's no problem," he says. "I haven't started it yet."

I tell him that I'm going to have a set of Carillos shipped on to him, and there is a long pause.

"How much they get for those things?" he says at last.

"Five hundred bucks," I tell him.

"Forget it."

"What's that?"

"I said, forget it. They're just not worth it. The rods you have look just fine, so let me put your mind to rest," he says. He seems a bit prickly that I've chosen not to heed what he told me earlier. He slows everything down, as if he's explaining something to a child.

"You can't break those seventy-four-inch rods. I've been souping these bikes up since before they even *made* eighty-inch connecting rods, and I'm here to tell you, you can't break the seventy-fours. Even running alcohol. Even on a hillclimber. So spend that five hundred dollars on something you really need."

"Okay, Ken," I tell him. "I'll put it all into chrome, then."

"*Now* you're talkin'," he says.

I hang up the phone and breathe a sigh of relief. There's something about talking to Ken that's reassuring, like talking to your dad. If your dad happens to be the reassuring kind.

Mine is not. Coincidentally, though, his name is also Ken.

Pop taught me how to change the oil in the lawn mower, how to gas and lube the garden tractor. When I became interested in model airplanes, we spent an afternoon at the basement workbench, trying to start my tiny 049 Wasp motor. We hooked up the battery, primed it, spun the prop. Nothing happened. We tried again. Nothing happened.

"I'm just no good at these things," my father said, and with that, he washed his hands of the project and I was on my own.

Afterward I tried to think of how long we might have spent, and while, at the time, it seemed like an entire afternoon, now I am thinking it was probably more like an hour. Nobody brought sandwiches and coffee down so we could keep working on it. Nobody said "We'll get this sucker going if it takes all night." It just seemed like a long time because it was probably about as long as I ever spent with Pop. I don't think the project interested him that much. I can't think of any project that interested him that much. Come to think of it, I don't think that *I* interested him that much.

Chaz and I talk more about what color I'll paint this Chief. We talk about red, we talk about black, then he tells me how "trashy-looking" a vintage bike can look when it's painted a contemporary color. He's telling me this because the week before I happened to see the graphic artist Steve LaRance's hot-rod Ford parked in front of Chaz's place and it was the most amazing shade of blue that I've ever seen—a kind of a midnight cobalt that looked to be three feet deep—a blue right out of my dreams.

"*Trust* me, Stroker," Chaz tells me. "You don't want to paint a classic bike a hot-rod color."

I know he's probably right, but it's too late. I've seen Millennium Blue, and it's stuck in my dreams.

The next morning Chaz and I have coffee at a sidewalk table at Second Thoughts Cafe, on the left bank of the Clark Fork River. These various coffee shops serve as a kind of floating office for Chaz, and in the course of the morning the whole spectrum of his acquaintances show up: a mechanic, a roofer, two contractors, and LaRance. They are all friends of Chaz's, and since they all own American V-twin motorcycles, they are all his customers, too.

I tell Chaz that Ken seemed almost insulted by the idea of my getting the heavier connecting rods, even though *he* was the guy who originally suggested it. I tell him Ken told me he'd never seen a broken 74-inch rod.

Chaz is having his morning eye-opener, which is four shots of espresso in a giant paper cup. All the waitresses in the café know this, and sometimes they even hand it to him as he walks in. Occasionally they even hang around to watch what happens when he drinks it.

Chaz grins at me over his quadruple shot, says, "Well, maybe *Ken* has never seen a broken seventy-four-inch connecting rod. But *I* sure have. Boy, they'll snap just like a pretzel. Have you seen one of those buggers? They're these really long, skinny, spindly-looking things."

"Wow," I say. "Why are you telling me this? *You* were the one who told me Ken was the only rebuild guy to go with. Now I've insulted him and you're telling me that, oh yeah, by the way, Ken could be off his rocker."

Here Chaz grows serious. He pats me gently on the shoulder in what I take as a fraternal gesture, and he says, "Listen, Fred. Don't fret about it. If Ken says those rods will hold, those rods will hold. Believe me, this kind of thing is going to be the *least* of your worries."

It's bright and cool out now, and the Grizzly footballers are down by the river in shorts and pads. When Caroline got her job at the magazine, she replaced a woman who quit because she was pregnant. Caroline's afraid they'll frown on the possibility of this happening again, so for now at least, at work the pregnancy is Top Secret, and each morning I'm asked the question, "Do I look too pregnant in this dress?" Finally I say, "Listen. You're just going to have to tell those people, Caroline."

Chaz comes by with a pickup load of junk from an old workshop he's cleaning out. He sells me a lawn mower for forty bucks. He's trying to get up enough cash to drive out to Portland and pick up the pair of

45ci Scouts, one of which he's already sold to Indian Mike, the eternal optimist.

I mow my lawn, change my clothes, and Caroline and I go on to a big garden party. I get into the gin for the first time this summer—immediately, all the women look terrific. And somewhere in the course of the evening, my friend Peter Stark and I resolve to go hunting in the Missouri Breaks this fall. Peter is a father too, but ten years younger. He is youthful, wiry, exuberant, a fine writer and an expert skier. He's talking about how rich this town seems to him. The gin works its magic and I tell him I think the town seems rich, too. His little daughter, Molly, is utterly charming, makes fatherhood look great. Everyone seems to like the name Caroline and I have decided on, Phoebe Rose. But mostly what happens this night is, the season passes and it is the first party of autumn.

Autumn again! I'm just about to let it get me down when Magoo calls to tell me my tanks are done. I drink a double latte, go down to the bank, and rack up another $500 on the old Gold Card—which I don't dare tell Caroline about. Then I run over to Magoo's. My tanks look terrific. Immaculate. Transformed. They're in gray primer with a slight olive tint. Magoo is more chatty than usual, maybe because I handed him $500 in cash. He says that a close inspection of my frame revealed it was in very good shape. "Much better than most," he said, though he shows me on the jig he's set up to align the seat-post tube to the steering head that it's "tweaked," off by a quarter of an inch. "You probably wouldn't even notice, but as long as we have it in there," he said, "let's go ahead and straighten it." He does this by putting a hydraulic girder against the seat-post tube and giving it a nudge.

Magoo tells me the only other things that need attention are a broken kick-start stop, the engine-mount hole, which he will fill and redrill, and the crash-bar indentations. We don't discuss price, because I want the frame to be as right as he can make it, but he tells me that if I don't go two-tone, he could paint my Chief for about $600.

I hurry home with my pristine set of tanks, which are now sitting in my office, on the carpet. They look so beautiful, I don't want to ever put gas in them. I don't even want to put them in my garage.

Chaz comes by, and we go down the street to Craig Eddy's house and look at his Indian. Craig is a heart surgeon who, legend has it, put himself through med school by moonlighting as a Harley mechanic. He has a beautiful white '46 Chief that is plagued by various gremlins. He thinks it might even be original—that is, unrestored. He's got a terrific-looking garage with several BSAs and a nice Panhead Harley he said he rode up the Bitterroot River Valley last night. I just stand there a moment in his garage and covet his bikes. It's a terrible thing to want that way, but when we leave, I tell Chaz I feel I really need a second motorcycle.

"No you don't, Stroker." He grins. "You just need a bike that *runs*."

CHAPTER 7

HUNTING THE BREAKS

Toward the end of October, the doctor tells Caroline we need to monitor the baby's movements—she should be sleeping up to forty minutes at a stretch, and moving two or three times an hour. This should be pretty easy for Phoebe, who is flipping around or hiccuping away in there nonstop. Dr. Richards said that the baby is now viable. That's the word she used—*viable,* as in "capable of living."

I haul my new forty-dollar mower out of the garage and prepare to cut our lawn for the last time this year. When I drag it out again in the spring, I will have a five-month-old baby girl.

The mower starts on the first pull, but a large chunk of the blade-housing hub breaks loose underneath, clatters around horribly, then bounces out and rolls to a stop at my feet. The engine races wildly, then almost dies. I don't want to stop it, because I cannot bring myself to deal with another crummy old piece of machinery, and since it still cuts, I resolve to mow with it as is. I discover I now have to yank the mower around violently in order to keep it running; to the casual passerby, I must look like a man who's lost his mind. But it sure beats sitting down and trying to fix it.

I finish mowing just before the rain sets in, and by evening it's snowing about a thousand feet up the mountain. Next door, the pair of sugar maples are blown bare and there's deer scat all around our crab apple tree. Last night I dreamed about a little whitetail buck, his antlers coiled, curled in, like a Big Horn ram's. I know I could be prepping the front forks and dealing with my wheels and brakes, but hunting season is upon us and motorcycling seems so far away.

By November the weather turns arctic, and the hunting pact I made with Peter Stark, way back in August, has finally come due. We planned to hunt the same stretch of river we canoed down over the summer, but I'm beginning to wonder if I have the gear for this kind of expedition. I've heard stories of parties getting frozen in on the Missouri as early as October, and a couple of friends who should know what they're talking about tell me we're crazy to set out this late. But finally, I can't let Peter call me a wimp. Can I?

We're late. We put in at Coal Banks Landing at four P.M., load Peter's eighteen-foot cargo canoe quickly but with a degree of care we didn't take last summer. It is very cold, in the single digits. Nobody mentions it, but it's clear that a spill in this water would be a disaster. Close to shore, the water is thickening, has that gelatinous look that precedes freezing, and there's a skiff of ice about fifteen feet long at our exit channel downstream. Hastily, we balance our load, secure it with bungie cords, and push off. We paddle hard into the ice, hoping to bust through it, but it's thicker than it looks and it slows us almost to a dead stop, so that we hack and chop frantically with our paddles just to keep going. But finally we hit the river's heavy current, which takes our canoe and seems to fling us downstream.

The plan is to paddle hard and get as far as we can before we put in for the night. The autumn light reflecting off the river is magnificent, startlingly clear. The cottonwoods are bare, the bench land is buff-colored, the river green, powerful, fast. I'm in the bow, and Peter is in the stern. With each stroke the temperature seems to drop, and I understand that inside of an hour or two, our situation could be serious, and that it will require all the attention and carefulness we can muster.

Around every bend, great flights of waterfowl rise before us by the thousands: mallards and wigeons, wood ducks and teal, Canada and snow geese, all driven downriver by the arctic front.

At the very end of the light, with the temperature still dropping, we finally head for shore, where Peter and I make camp with a quiet urgency. There's plenty of deadwood scattered around, so I abandon our Coleman, go with an open fire and a folding grate, cook our pasta puttanesca. We eat quickly, then scour the cottonwood groves, build the fire up, then settle in close with Oreos and whiskey. Coincidentally, Peter and I both wear brand-new forest-green wool pants with razor creases, which give the bivouac a goofy kind of elegance. With the flashlight on Peter's thermometer we see that it's five degrees, and it seems like such an accomplishment, just pitching the tent and feeding ourselves, that we finally stop thinking about being frozen in that night.

Peter tells me about the family bed—the current theory that it's healthier, more natural, for the whole family to sleep together in a common bed. He says they've done this forever in Bali, that they talk about westerners putting their babies "in cages."

"So, do you guys do the family bed?"

"Oh, sure," says Peter.

"You're kidding me."

"No," he says. "Really."

"Boy," I tell him. "Does *that* ever sound busy."

Later, it starts to make sense, especially on a night like this, freezing cold and wild. Coyotes yip somewhere up on the bench, a skin of ice spreads out from the banks, while chevrons of geese honk across the full moon. The frost in the air and on the grass is brilliant, jewel-like in the moonlight, and the campground, the river seem enchanted. We stay up to watch the crystalline night as the temperature continues to drop.

By the time we turn in it's close to zero. We climb into our winter tent and our state-of-the-art sleeping bags with our jackets, hats, and gloves on. We plan to shed the outerwear as soon as we warm up, but we never do. Even in that expedition tent in hi-tech bags, we merely break even. It is a terribly restless night. Sometime before dawn, I have a terrifying attack of claustrophobia, kick free of the bag, wake up gasping as the thought flickers across my mind that I've just now dreamed my birth experience.

Through the tent fly I can see steam rising from the river, hear the geese calling, while beside me, Peter snores like a turbine. I wonder if the dawn will bring us a frozen river and a long walk back.

In a couple of minutes, Peter yawns, scratches, sits up in his bag. The walls of the tent are covered with ice. He blinks, turns to me with a grin. "Man," he says. "You were *really* snoring."

In western Montana, the lodgepole pine gets so thick and dark that, even with a compass, I never quite shake my fear that I'll get turned around. While we break camp and pack the tent, I understand that it's not unlike my biggest fear of this Indian restoration—that somehow in taking this bike all apart, I will fail to mark my bearings and I'll never get it back together. But the Breaks are in the east. They're virtually treeless, wide open, expansive, and the last thing you worry about is where you've been.

We have some good luck and it warms to nearly twenty degrees. The sun comes out. A mile or so downstream from camp, I take a shot at a white-tail doe from the bow of the canoe. It makes me feel stupid, like a roadhunter, but that's mostly because I miss. Peter holds the canoe steady enough, but using my knees for a shooting rest is a bum technique. I experiment, find it's much steadier when I lie down in the bow and use the gunwales as a bench. Now there are great flocks of birds, thousands of waterfowl, but no more deer.

We put in at Lewis and Clark's May 31 camp in the early afternoon, hunt the bench and coulees behind us till nightfall, but there's not an animal to be seen. At one point I venture out onto a sandstone promontory, look way downriver, then back the way we came.

I was watching television at my best friend's apartment when my first marriage finally broke in two. The 1968 Chicago Democratic Convention was on, my wife was out of town, my best friend was out of town, and I was watching the coverage with his wife. With Vietnam boiling over, the assassinations of King and Robert Kennedy in the spring, and the riots and uprisings of the summer, it was a year that should have inured us to almost anything, and yet, the two of us discovered, it had not. We sat there stupefied by the panorama of clubbings, gassings, and mayhem that continued on into the night, even spilled over into the studio, with Gore Vidal and William F. Buckley clawing each other's eyes out. I looked at my friend's wife and she looked at me, and everything ground to a stop. We had marched against the war, all of us. We'd gone to countless rallies and we'd got Clean for Gene, but in the eye of that moment, the two of us realized that it didn't matter anymore what you did or didn't do. The world had gone mad. Everything was flying apart. Everything was hopelessly broken. Then we gave ourselves up to this, my good friend's wife and I. Within minutes, we were in their bed, the two of us breaking the last of the things unbroken with a joyless, doomed kind of lovemaking that would leave us haunted for years.

Already under strain, my marriage now began to founder. I couldn't fix it, did not care to try. My wife took my daughter and left for Italy, while I stayed home to get myself together. Before the semester was up, I'd left graduate school and taken to the trees.

In leftist Cambridge, with my Bohemian friends talking about "the workers," it pleased me to think that I was the only one of them who actually *was* a worker. And not just some factory stiff but a high climber, a taker of big risks.

It was a perfectly good way to romanticize myself, but mostly I was a man haunted by the failure of his marriage, and the general failure of himself as a person, and with the war grinding on, it was a great relief to be too tired or too preoccupied with survival to think very much. I gave myself up to the demands of tree work as I had never done with anything else. I learned to rope up the great eastern black oaks, to balance in a crotch with a saw revving full bore, and in a year or two, when I was finally good enough, I came to work with hair down to my shoulders and a Fritz the Cat T-shirt. The rednecks I worked with spit and glared, but I didn't give a damn. I could outclimb any of them and they knew it. For the first time in my life I knew how to *do* something.

I see now that the trees were a willful kind of devolution, a way of reinventing myself by going all the way back to the beginning. A way to learn all the life lessons that had eluded me so far, the lessons of fellowship and hard work—and particularly, the lessons of courage. In spite of my posturing, my life in the trees had nothing to do with correct politics. The trees were where I would go until I became the person I wanted to be, *needed* to be, to see my son again.

By noon the next day it's warmed into the thirties. We're drifting with the current, eating sardines, when Peter spots white-cleft mule deer rumps, high on the north shore. Immediately, we drop our lunches, paddle till we're out of their line of sight, put in, and ascend the downstream side of a coulee.

We climb fast, two, three hundred feet to the top of the coulee. We're breathing hard. We're hunting in a magnificent gold light and the country around us is superb. We peek over the rise, and the mulies aren't where they should be. Instead, they are just uphill—a handsome pair of bucks, scrambling up the scree. Peter and I flop down on our bellies, and I wait for him to squeeze one off. The bucks are up against a six-foot sandstone wall, and there's no place for them to go but downhill. And then, incredibly, the two deer stand erect, throw their forelegs onto the sandstone mantle, and with a couple of kicks of their strong hind legs, muscle right up the wall. My God, I think. I didn't know they could do *that*! Meantime, Peter has forgotten to turn off his safety—that's why he doesn't shoot—and I jerk off a shot in frustration just as the mulies bolt straight uphill.

Peter and I follow them higher, catch a small herd on very steep scree that funnels off to the ridgeline. The big bucks scent us, nearly trample the rest of the herd to get out of there. Again we drop to our stomachs, and this time Peter takes a spikehorn buck with a spinal shot while I drop a plumpish-looking doe with a heart shot. At last! A decent shot!

It's Peter's first kill, so I let him dress both the animals while I wander off to admire the country. Fifty yards away, I glance back just as Peter crouches over his buck, takes a bite of something red and dripping. It's funny and kind of startling, too, and I think, Jesus, I didn't know I was sharing a tent with a guy like *that*. . . .

But now we have to get our animals back downhill. Far below us we can see the canoe, beached alongside a creek outlet, and Peter says, "How did we get so *high*?"

We huff and puff, finally drape the deer over our shoulders, pack them off on the long downhill hike like old-time mountain men—we haven't seen another human being in nearly three days. We're back on the river by four, and of course we see big mulie bucks the rest of the way down, till shooting light fades.

In celebration, Peter roasts Cornish hens on a spit that night while we have an extra bourbon before dinner. By the light of the moon you can see our two deer, packed side by side in the Mad River canoe, their profiles rigid, sightless, skyward, like some ancient pharaoh and his queen.

The next day the wind picks up and the Missouri gets rough. The canoe rolls in the swells, and at least once we ship water over the gunwales. By the time we put in at Judith Landing, the wind is fierce. When the old man comes from the Fort Benton shuttle service to pick us up, he inspects our animals, says, "Well. You got *some*thing, anyway." He looks a little closer at Peter's spikehorn and says, "Gosh. I guess they'll let you shoot about anything these days."

But Peter and I don't care. Sure, we could have taken bigger animals and we certainly could have shot better. But it was a fine adventure on a magnificent river. It was exactly the kind of adventure I always dreamed of, growing up in Michigan.

Magoo calls to tell me he needs my steering-head bearings in order to fit my frame on his straightening jig. I run over with a box of front-end parts, which Magoo tells me contains no steering-head bearings at all. I feel stupid for not knowing this, but Magoo says it doesn't matter, that he has some extras around somewhere.

My frame is standing on its nose, tail in the air. Magoo is under his welding hood, smoothing out the chewed-up front sections with his torch. I have a six-pack of Oktoberfest Brew in my truck and we crack a couple, discuss my options for a rusty but genuine Indian front wheel.

Rechroming has become prohibitively expensive—in California it costs twice as much to rechrome an old one as it does to buy a new one. Magoo says these rims can be painted, but then I'd have to paint my rear rim, which is an alloy, to match, and alloy doesn't hold paint well. Then, since nobody seems to do cadmium plating anymore, there is always a zinc wash, but that tends to look too yellow. Starklite wants 90 bucks for new spokes, 80 bucks to lace and true them, 80 bucks for a new chrome rim—250 bucks total. Magoo says that this is the hard part of a restoration—all the calculations and trade-offs. Should you scrimp on the wheels to spend more on the motor? The problem with restorations is, you never know what you should have done until the bike is finished.

We talk for a moment about the paint job. Magoo says that while a lot of people go with the flashier two-tone color schemes, solid colors were the rule for the postwar Chiefs, and that I can add a couple of thousand to my restoration value, just by using the correct color and ornamentation.

I tell Chaz I think I'll go ahead and have the guys in Bozeman rechrome my original Indian rim, that they'll do it for half the price of the California outfits.

Chaz is skeptical. "We've been through this a thousand times, Fred. I can't believe you're going to use a henhouse outfit like Bozeman, where they'll be sure to fuck it up. Why don't you just buy a new rim and spokes?"

I tell him that Bootsy told Magoo Bozeman's chrome plate looked pretty good.

Chaz scowls. "Oh, *fuck* Bootsy!"

We go on in this manner for a while. It seems like the whole issue here involves a loyalty to original parts, and while I let that be the determining factor with my tanks, I'm beginning to understand that if I keep on like this I will shortly be out of money. Besides, I'm tired of arguing with Chaz, so I decide to change the subject.

"So, Chaz. Should I go with whitewalls or not?"

"That depends," he says thoughtfully. "How slutty do you want your bike to be?"

We are planning to go bid a largish tree job, but Magoo calls to tell me my frame is ready, and somehow we end up out there instead.

My frame looks marvelous. Very black, so shiny it looks wet, it sits in Magoo's drying room in front of the old Parts Father logo.

Magoo has Harley fenders and a gas tank on his drying rack. They are a stunning ruby red that he says is candy apple over gold. They look ten miles deep. Magoo says they might look good on an Indian, but after I see my frame I begin to think that maybe this whole bike wants to be that wonderful shiny bottomless black.

As usual, I end up back in my garage. I'm sitting on my pickup seat, staring at my shiny black frame beneath a hundred-watt lightbulb. The wind's blowing hard outside and Caroline's at a baby shower up the street. I don't know how I'll ever finish this project and I don't know what possessed me to ever take it on. I don't even know how we'll get through the winter, especially with a baby on the way.

But here's what I *do* know: that somehow I've given myself up to all this. The Chief is in the driver's seat now, and you've got to be ready to go where the Chief wants to take you.

CHAPTER 8

THE FAMILY BED

By December the big winds arrive. There's a full moon the night of the sixth, and early this morning I am awakened by a huge bang out in front of the house. Is it a sonic boom or is it just a gust on that goofy sheet-metal canopy over our front door? If only we could buy this house, the first thing I would do would be to rip that canopy right off. Unfortunately, though, we can't afford to buy it. You could make the case that we can't afford to buy it because of this dumb-ass motorcycle project, but Caroline is a remarkably good sport about it all. The other night at a party, a friend said she thought that Caroline was having an "extremely graceful pregnancy," and I looked over at Caroline then, at the elegant drape of her black cocktail dress, at the way she sipped sparkling cider from a champagne glass. I don't know if it's the same as grace, but she looked lit up and happy in a way I've never seen her before.

The radio says the winds are hurricane force, seventy-five mph plus. The temperature is in the single digits, there are big trees down all over town, and this morning the phone begins to ring.

On the way to our first bid, Chaz tries to soften me up enough to sell me a '71 Volkswagen camper.

I tell him I'm not interested. It gets annoying, the way he still doesn't realize I'm at least as broke as he is.

He says something like, "You and your missus, you guys are outdoor types. Now, why would folks like yourselves *not* have a camper?"

"I dunno, Chaz. Because we don't *want* one?"

"Well, maybe it's just because you haven't seen *this* one. . . ."

Really, sometimes spending the day with Chaz is like being trapped with a life insurance guy.

Our first is a seventy-foot triple-headed spruce, blown over onto a very fragile-looking maple, which, in turn, overhangs a two-story house. I look at it from every angle. I see cats and crows everywhere. I think, Ah, the *hell* with this screwball tree business, and I call the owner and bid it at twice what it's worth. The good news is, I get the job. The bad news is, now I have to *do* it.

By the end of the week I've done more spring poles, bastard traps, and widowmakers than I have in years. We've finally got our Christmas money, but I'm feeling beat up and dragged out most of the time.

By the sixth meeting of our childbirthing class, I have to drink a latte just to make it over there. On the way over I'm nearly broadsided by two kids in a lightless van, hurtling down a side street at about fifty miles per hour. We both swerve, skid to a stop, and stall out, right there in front of the midwife's house. I bail out of our Subaru, swinging mad. I call this kid every name I can think of, but the expletive I keep coming back to is "pissant." I love the ring of "Pissant!" in the cold night air, in the middle of the empty street, the blood hot in my veins.

The kid stands there and takes it, like he's waiting out a rain squall or something, and it feels great to holler and carry on.

Tonight in our birthing class, the midwife shows slides. Caroline and I kick off our shoes and sit cross-legged among the beanbags with a handsome tie-dyed couple from down the street. They appear to be about the same age as my daughter, Sara, but who's keeping score?

We watch lots of slides and movies of births, and I begin to notice that without exception all the guys in these movies have beards, and I begin to wonder if it's OK to show up at my daughter's birth clean-shaven. At the end of class we work a breathing technique they call the Heehee-hoo. Involving two quick inhalations and a long exhalation, Heehee-hooing is reserved for the difficult "transition" phase of labor, but the Heehee-hoo is somehow contagious, and I find myself doing it all the way home.

We bid on a couple of newer woodlot homes east of town that have sustained major storm damage, and the Douglas firs are down everywhere. Funny, I always thought of them as a powerfully rooted tree, but they're jackstrawed every which way, like so many spruce. There's a long one lying across a garage, and somebody is going to have to shinny fifty feet out on it, cut the brush off, and whittle the log back, all the time bouncing up and down like a yo-yo. Unfortunately, that somebody is me.

"You get a camper like this one," Chaz says, "Caroline takes the baby, you take the bike, and the three of you go anywhere in the Northwest. Then, when you want to call it a day, just pull into the old campground and pop up the top."

He's still trying to sell me this camper even when we get home, but over a cup of coffee in my kitchen, there gets to be some uncomfortable "kidding on the square" about who really owes whom in this partnership. I realize it has to do with a commission I took from a job I threw his way and that he's miffed because he thinks it was too much. This is the first time I've seen Chaz really keep score, and while I know that it's Christmas and his family needs money, I find I'm not particularly interested in hearing about it—mostly because I'm already paying him twice what I ever paid anyone and he doesn't even climb.

For a while we do a funny little dance—full of puffery and semi-mock indignation, which, ultimately, seems to have to do with nickels and dimes. I realize, finally, that a gesture needs to be made, and I pull a twenty-dollar bill out of my jeans. I don't even know what it's for, but I wave it around until Chaz finally goes to *his* pocket, pulls out a ten, waves that around. Then we swap bills and call it a night. Chaz is no sooner out the door than my father calls.

My father is ninety years old, and he and my stepmother are in the process of moving from North Carolina to a retirement community near Savannah. I imagine he's calling to tell me how the move is going, but instead he's calling to tell me that he's not sure his pacemaker is working right, because he fell and broke his collarbone.

"My God, when was that, Pop?"

"Well, let's see. It must have been right after I got out of prostate surgery, Fred. But anyway, I wanted to tell you that's the reason why your Christmas present will be a little bit late."

"*Jesus,* Pop!" I tell him. "Why don't you tell me when this stuff happens?"

"Well," he says, shyly. "I just didn't want to bother you, Fred."

"Well, do you want me to come out there?"

"No."

"Well, okay, Pop. I hope you feel better."

I have tried for fourteen years, roughly since his second marriage, to stay a good deal closer to my father. But again and again, he's brushed aside my invitations for him to visit. And he has never actually invited us to visit him. The couple times we *did* visit uninvited were tense enough to cause him to remark that perhaps traveling out to see him wasn't a particularly wise use of our money. Over the years he's told me I was crazy to try to write, crazy to go to Stanford, and most recently, crazy to become a father at this point in my life (which he actually told me before, when I was in my early twenties). Essentially, he has treated anything I've ever cared about as a kind of joke. So how Pop can set up this stiff-arm distance and still expect guilt to work is baffling. I hang up the phone as always—clueless about what my father expects from his son.

I'm simultaneously sorry for and angry with Pop, yet for some reason I'm still thinking about Chaz. Somehow, Chaz seems to be more and more like family all the time.

This whole family bed business has seeped into my consciousness since I first heard about it on the banks of the Missouri, and I believe we need to address the question of where we'll all sleep. The double bed we've been sleeping in for ten years is shot—dished out on one side, rock hard on the other—and since I'm six feet three, there never was much room in there anyway. Tiny babies have a way of winding up in bed with their mothers, and I want to get a bed we can all fit into. We can't really afford a new bed. Then again, if it isn't motorcycle parts, we can't afford much of anything. Still, since sleep will be at a premium the next several months, I've made up my mind this is something we should have and I start shopping.

There is probably nothing in the world as dreary as a furniture store, and in a week's time I've been to many. I have a clear picture of the three of us snuggled deep beneath our eiderdown while it blows fifty below out there, and I can't shake it loose, even though I know they call this behavior "nesting." I pursue this bed doggedly, haunting the discount showrooms of Missoula for the queen-size of my dreams.

Meanwhile, Caroline has nesting projects of her own. She's decided to paint the baby's room and the kitchen, too, and for weeks all the silverware and dishes are in the dining room. Our house is torn up in a way I haven't seen since we moved in, and in a larger sense, it's all for the sake of the family bed.

Christmas comes and goes in a blur. Even though her arrival date is still three weeks away, Phoebe gets more presents than any of us. My brother Marc flies in from L.A. with presents for us: single malt whiskey, Trader Joe's coffee, and a CD featuring Yo-Yo Ma and Bobby McFerrin collaborating on "Mockingbird."

My brother wants to see the Chief immediately, so I take him to the garage, switch on the light. I show him the freshly primed gas tanks, the glossy black frame, and a pair of Japanese knockoffs of the Goodyear Speed-Grip tire (unmounted). It's funny—when I see this stuff, I see a project well on its way. But my brother, well, for just a second I see a flicker of sadness cross his face, as if he's reflecting on his kid brother's boundless capacity for optimism and self-delusion.

Missoula is Planet Smog. We're into our annual worst weather of the year, and it's quite horrible to look at out there. Last night I dreamed that Ken Edmiston called to tell me that my motor was ready, and then I was *there,* materialized in his shop, where he was just pulling something out of the oven. It was like a big cookie in the shape of a clutch pedal, and it was still warm, fragrant with the smell of freshly baked rubber. He grinned as he presented it to me, and he told me that he "did about forty-eight of these a year."

Caroline and I can't quite finish with the house. We move more stuff all around, prepare to paint the baby's room but then somehow never get around to it. Yesterday we finally consummated our search for a family bed: a queen-size Sealy at a warehouse store west of town. The mattresses were stacked up against the wall, and to see what we were getting, Caroline and I pulled one down and stretched out on it in the middle of the store with a hundred passersby. Then we bought it, dragged it outside, lashed it to the car roof like it was something I'd shot, and drove home with our last Big Ticket Item of 1995.

New Year's Day our house is still ripped up. It has been for as long as anyone can remember. It takes forever to get the baby's room and bedroom all emptied out, and then, once we do this, nobody can remember why we felt it was necessary in the first place. I'm tired and crabby, and I paint for a while, then take off to the Montana Legends Annual New Year's Ride at the Iron Horse Pub.

The Montana Legends is a loosely organized group of cyclists from around the state who, as one of them put it, "don't care much about football and really like to ride." The Annual New Year's Ride is held whatever the weather, and most of the cyclists hearty enough to participate do so with madcap enthusiasm: There is one biker with a dinner jacket on over his leathers. Another biker in full clown suit on a flaming minibike. Lots of bikers with Hawaiian shirts over leathers—this might even be the official Legends Outfit—but my favorite is the guy in the motocross pants, World War II leather jacket with a PLO shemagh, and Shriners fez. Many of the cyclists rode their beaters, but I see a couple of Chiefs, including Dave Warhank on a rough-looking 1941 and Artie, from Coeur d'Alene, on a 1946, the one with the '52 Blackhawk motor. His wife Elisa is there with her Sport Scout, but it's still in primer. There is a Whizzer motorized bicycle, a couple of Russian Urel sidecar rigs. But it's spectacular when they all start up and ride off. *That's* when you feel really left out, and sick and crabby as I was, I still wanted to ride off with the Legends. I follow them out to Harold's Club in Milltown, drink a beer with Magoo and Artie, who wins a trophy for Best Indian. His wife wins a trophy for Oldest Indian. Artie is talking to another Indian rider, who also has an 80-incher, one he stroked himself. Like me, he's running S&S flywheels with stock 74-inch rods. I express my concern about this combination.

"Hey," he says. "Long as you're not popping wheelies all the time, they'll do you just fine."

We're standing around, all of us, behind the venerable Harold's Club, where there's beer and laughter and motor talk, and then around three o'clock a big flight of geese passes over us, heading downstream. Suddenly everything stops, and everyone watches in utter silence.

Phoebe's due date is upon us. The weekly checkup reveals that the cervix is "thinning," not dilating, so we'll just keep hanging on. The air is less smoggy, but the sky is leaden. During a thaw, Chaz and I go out to take away a blown-down apricot on Fifth Street. Immediately, it seems, we get on each other's nerves. He complains that there's too much brush, not enough money. We begin to argue about all kinds of things—particularly, how to load a truck. The friendship, or whatever it is, is unraveling before my eyes. I get sullen and very quiet, which is my way.

Chaz picks up on it and backs off. "So," he asks. "What are you thinking?"

"Hey. You don't want to know," I tell him, but I'm thinking that, at the rate we're going, this partnership won't last another week.

In an attempt to keep things afloat, we head to Second Thoughts for coffee, where I sit for a while as Chaz rattles on about something I'm not really listening to. All I can think about is how hard winter is going to be, who else I can get to help me in the trees, and who else I can get to help me with this bike. Suddenly I'm aware the conversation has changed: I hear him say something about "Zoloft."

"What about Zoloft?" I say.

"Like I was saying, it's supposed to be the Thinking Man's Prozac."

The winter before, my situation seemed desperate. Somehow I had squandered all my opportunities. Somehow I had mismanaged myself badly, and my careers as a writer and a teacher were both dead in the water. I became obsessive, dark, and withdrawn. One of my favorite late-night pastimes became cleaning my .357 pistol. If Caroline had not had enough of it all and talked me into finding help, I might never have survived.

"Wait a minute," I say. "What do you know about Zoloft?"

"Oh man," he says. "I was taking that stuff all autumn."

It's too much, the sheer coincidence of it all—the two struggling middle-aged men, up to their eyeballs in babies, motorcycles, and anti-depressants. It finally breaks the ice, and I grin and blurt out, "But that's *my* medication!"

And once again, the friendship has survived.

That night, Caroline and I finally take the Christmas tree down. We're lying in our new family bed, in our newly painted rooms, and I'm reading the Starklite Indian catalogue to see how many parts I'm missing from my front end. Caroline is reading *Stones from the River*. She says it's really good, and I'm jealous and wish I weren't hung up in a damn parts catalogue again. She tells me that on the way to work she heard a Phoebe in the alley.

Later on Caroline rolls back and forth—she's having some kind of Braxton Hicks' contractions. She gets sweaty, crampy. I put my hand on her stomach, and the baby is flipping around like a gymnast. There's movement galore, but still nothing happens, and I go to sleep dreaming, for some reason, about my father.

CHAPTER 9

WAITING FOR PHOEBE

By mid-January, Phoebe's due date has come and gone. I'm having coffee with Chaz one morning and he says, "These next few weeks? Hey, Stroker. I wouldn't be in your shoes for a million bucks."

It's so smoky, foggy, and crummy, I don't blame my baby a bit for being slow to come out. If I were Phoebe, I'd stay put just as long as I could.

To pass the time Caroline and I watch a lot of movies. From the sublime (*Pride and Prejudice, Quiz Show, Apollo 13*) to the ridiculous (*Where the Boys Are*), and a dozen others I can't remember. One night we are so desperate for something to watch, we finally break out the child-birthing movies we got from Dolly Browder—the ones we should have watched already but haven't. More guys with beards. Why it is these home-birth dads are always unshaven remains puzzling, but the movies seem brave and joyous, and we both weep as baby after baby corkscrews his way out, into this mysterious and dangerous place the Buddhists call "the Phenomenal World."

Caroline dreamed she went to a strange new doctor who was able to show her computer-generated pictures of the way Phoebe will look maybe twenty years from now. Caroline says the pictures showed a willowy young woman with a great big smile and long dark hair. Me, I had another dream about my phantom son. In this dream he's finally about the right age and we finally meet up by some computer terminal in inner space. Beyond that I can't remember much, except that we both seemed relieved to finally get *that* out of the way.

Sometimes we try to imagine what Phoebe will be like, but of course, it is beyond us. Not like the Chief, where all I have to do is pick a color, decide on whitewalls or not. Caroline worries about me getting the two of them mixed up, but the other day in the doctor's office, it was Caroline, not me, who said the baby's heartbeat sounded like a little motor.

Caroline is a powerhouse right now. She zips around cleaning the house, finishing old freelance editing projects. Her balance is great, her stamina is superb, and except for the problems posed by bending over, she moves amazingly well for someone carrying an extra forty pounds. She likes to lie in the bathtub now with her Crabtree & Evelyn bubble bath. Her favorite scents are peach and honeysuckle. She likes to lie back in the suds and watch Phoebe move around in her stomach. She'll do that for an hour at a time, and sometimes I hear her talking while she watches that baby like a cat. More than anything, I like watching Caroline watch the baby.

Last night we try again to get Phoebe to come out. (The only problem with letting her stay is that she might get too big to come out on her own.) Here are some of the things we try: wine, beer, raspberry tea. A pizza called a Belly Buster, a brisk walk, a ride on a bumpy road where I aim for the chuckholes, and a couple more things I can't remember. Basically, we try every bit of folklore or old wives' tale we know. We continue to seek out the bumpiest roads in the Upper Rattlesnake Valley, and we run the old Subaru hard. All this so we can finally have a look at her.

Phoebe receives another present this evening—a tiny pair of red sneakers, which make her a candidate for best-dressed girl on the block before she's even born.

All this waiting has the effect of calming me down—at least in comparison to last week. Now I'm back to asking the really hard questions, like: Should I paint the Chief a solid color or should I go with a two-tone?

At night I go to the front door to let the dog out and there are seven, eight mule deer browsing under the crab apple. Instantly they're gone. Four run west, four run east. The dog is so startled, she doesn't even bark.

Over coffee next morning I ask Chaz about leathers.

"So, Chaz. What about leathers?"

"They're a real good idea."

"What about glitzy-ass biker designers like that outfit out of Sante Fe—would you say they're a sure sign of the gentrification of the sport?"

Chaz blinks. "I dunno."

We have another cup and then we're talking about accidents. I tell him about my great tunnel slide; he tells me about a guy who puts a cheap tire on the back of his 45ci Harley, loads it up with camping gear, blows the tire outside of Havre, and puts the bike in a borrow pit. He's covered with gas and burning like a torch. Passersby stop and put him out, but what does he do? He goes right back to the borrow pit to extinguish his bike and he catches fire again! This time they have to chopper him out to a burn center.

There's another story about a guy who pulls off the highway late at night, puts his foot down on the edge of the shoulder, and steps in a hole. His Harley falls over on him, pins him in the ditch with the red hot pipe to his leg.

We finish our muffins, and Chaz says with great seriousness, "I tell you these stories for a *reason,* Fred."

"I know that," I tell him, "I know that."

We're getting half a dozen calls a day about the baby, so I finally put a message on our tape telling people Phoebe hasn't arrived yet. Late one evening, Yvonne calls. "Chaz told me not to call you guys, but I couldn't stand it. Have you tried fennel-seed tea? Have you tried castor oil? We're thinking about you. . . ."

Caroline has cramps again, but the doctor says she is not yet beginning to dilate and we spend the rest of the afternoon at the clinic. Caroline is on the nonstress fetal monitor and Phoebe's little heartbeat comes in loud and clear, from about 130 to 150 beats per minute. Caroline logs her movements in with a clicker. Phoebe moves a lot, but sometimes she's quiet for several minutes at a time. It's clear that she's sleeping. Napping, I think. In the womb. And dreaming, too? What in the world do babies dream of? The place they just came from? The place they're on the way to? And what in the world is it like, preparing to be born? The doctor decides that Phoebe will be born sometime tomorrow.

The night before we go to the hospital we listen to President Clinton's State of the Union Address, then Senator Dole's response. The Senator is unnervingly sinister-looking, and the camera eases in close while he says, "Tonight, when you go down the hall to tuck in that brand-new baby, think about the future. Think about what kind of world that baby will be growing up in. Think about the promises being made by Bill Clinton that he can't ever hope to keep. Think about tax-and-spend liberals, then think about the heyday of the eighties . . ."

I decide to go outside before I get sick. I gas the car, pack the little bags we made up weeks ago, and before I go to bed I watch the weather. It looks like Phoebe waited for the biggest snowstorm and the coldest day of the winter to be born.

We arrive at the hospital at seven A.M. On our way to the delivery room, the nurses joke about how full of placentas the refrigerator is getting. They punch the petocin IV in Caroline's arm, and in the next few hours we have a series of three different nurses—a somber one, a heavy one, an edgy one—till we finally get the happy one. Of all the music tapes we've brought, the only one I play is Martin Denny's *Exotica,* a collection of '50s lounge music, and Caroline laughs so hard it hurts her and we have to turn it off.

I remember Caroline in the transition phase, the way the contractions crashed over her like huge waves while we locked on to each other's eyes. It's like my scuba-diving class, when we used to practice buddy breathing at the bottom of Monterey Bay. For the first time I can remember, I see that Caroline's afraid, and we breathe together, just the two of us: heehee-hooo, just like our lives depend on it.

After Phoebe enters the canal, Caroline's athleticism is superb, and toward the end it seems she's all over the delivery room as she squats and pushes, lies back down, pushes some more until, sometime around eight that evening, the child finally slides clear, and there is little Phoebe, who never really makes a sound. She just lies there quietly, so alert, bright-eyed, and watchful.

In the course of Phoebe's first night on earth she runs a temperature and the nurses get alarmed, and by the time I get back in the morning, they've done a spinal tap and about a hundred blood tests, she has a little antibiotics catheter planted in her scalp like a dreadlock, and they want to keep her in there for five days' observation. I am terribly worried, and angry, too. Nobody even bothered to call me, I suppose because it was the middle of the night. But what had they *done* to Phoebe while I was gone?

So I continue to spend my nights home alone with the animals, my parts catalogues, my Warthog Ales, and the evening dose of World War II on the television.

I wake to find the newspaper, which seems particularly full of mayhem this winter: an attack on two nuns in Maine, another prison murder, and—most bizarre—the billionaire John Du Pont has gone insane and shot a wrestler. It's funny, this whole tradition of newspapers: how the first thing you see every morning are your worst fears, in big capital letters, delivered oven-fresh from some nightmare factory to your door.

What Phoebe *was* waiting for was the coldest January in twenty years. The windchill temperatures are sixty below zero, and even with a block heater, folks can't start their motors. There's so much snow, we have to use four-wheel drive to go anywhere, even on the flats. The streets are drifted over and the air is so clear and the snow so bright that the town looks like some arctic refuge. The mountains in the Rattlesnake Wilderness stand out like the Brooks Range. It's the kind of winter I always knew this town had in it. The mulies on the hillsides look stricken and the waxwings plunder our mountain ash for berries, while down the alleyways, Phoebe birds call back and forth. The air freezes your cheeks in seconds, and it's just about as far from motorcycle weather as it could ever get.

That's the way it is when we finally bring Phoebe home. She has her last course of antibiotics around eleven P.M. and we triple-bundle her, strap her in her little car seat, toss a blanket over her, and spirit her in the back door near midnight.

The pets are flabbergasted. The dog keeps sniffing and sniffing, as if Phoebe doesn't quite make sense, but the cat just keeps his distance and watches. And from that night until she turns six months old, Phoebe sleeps with her dog and her cat, her mother and father in the brand-new family bed.

All through January and into February, I work on the Chief's wheels. Rechroming the original rim seems so expensive, I decide to buy a new one and lace in new stainless spokes from Starklite. I ask Frank if the Italian steel rim, which costs twice as much as the Taiwanese rim, is worth the extra money.

"Not really," says Frank.

And with that I disassemble the front wheel, send the hub down to California, have them replace the bearings and lace on a Taiwanese rim.

On the rear wheel, the alloy one, everything looks good, so I decide to rebuild it myself. Late on a Saturday night, I bang the old bearings out with a broom handle and a hard-rubber mallet while my electric furnace buzzes away, catching the scent of ancient wheel grease, wafting it through my garage. More potent than tea and madeleines, in a heartbeat the scent of grease takes me back to that great boyhood Hall of Mysteries I used to roam free in, the Henry Ford Museum in Dearborn, Michigan.

When I remember that place—the massive Allegheny steam locomotive, the Ford Trimotor that Admiral Byrd flew over the North Pole, the gigantic steam-driven tractors, and the great ranks of machines and automobiles that inhabited my boyhood and defined this century—I wonder what will end up being *your* Hall of Mysteries, Phoebe. Will it be a museum somewhere in cyberspace? And what machines will define your century, which will be an entirely different century than my own?

I wonder what vehicle she'll have to take her on the kind of journey I take with the Chief. And I wonder what little things she'll find packed away in her subconscious to tug at her memory like gravity. I wonder which bits of flotsam from her past, otherwise known as my present—will speak to her most eloquently.

By February I've taken the front fork apart, scraped it down, and it's ready for the paint shop. Things look pretty much the same as they have for a couple months, except that over in the corner, under the bare bulb, alongside the primered gas tanks and freshly painted frame, there is now a brilliant, shiny pair of motorcycle wheels, the spokes laced and trued, the tires mounted and balanced, the whitewalls still blue, as if from the cold.

CHAPTER 10

PARTS WARS

By the beginning of February the skies are blown open, the ground is frozen solid as an asteroid. The snow in the streets is polished and slick and the Clark Fork River is reduced to the span of a driveway as it plunges, dark and smoking, through the center of town.

It's twenty-five below these nights, and during the days we're still kept indoors, despite the sun's brightness. The animals wear the heavy coats of an epic winter and loll on the bare floors, while Caroline and I watch our milk-drunk baby nursing, yawning, and drifting in and out of some hibernation dream or winter trance-state. We dream, too—about the color of Phoebe's eyes and the way she'll look when she's older and of the fabulous machine I've begun that sits waiting for me in my garage.

A few days earlier, I'd gone by Chaz's to show him the new tires that had just come in.

His son Aydyn is cooing on his back as Chaz handles one

brusquely, gives it the once-over, and says, "Huh. A Speed-Grip. And you wouldn't buy one from me, you prick."

With his dealer's designation, Chaz can order parts at a low enough price so that he can make a few dollars on the order and the customer can still come out ahead of straight retail. But his comment brings me up short—first, because the kidding-on-the-square etiquette through which we generally speak our minds has been dispensed with; second, because as Chaz himself had to admit, I tried to order tires through him several weeks earlier and he never got around to putting the order in.

So when he calls a few days later to ask where I'm planning to buy my fenders, I hesitate.

"I don't know," I tell him.

"Well, why don't you buy them through me, Stroker?"

"Well. How much you think they will run me?"

Chaz snorts. "I can't tell you that until you actually *order* them. I mean, are you serious here or are we just screwing around?"

"Oh, I get it," I tell him. "You're saying that what they're going to cost me is none of my business?"

There is a rapid exchange of not so lighthearted gibes and insults, and then I hang up the phone, furious with him again. And though I know in my gut it's largely a product of Chaz's new baby and the kind of desperation that accompanies a Missoula winter, I want to quit this crumbling association while Chaz and I are still on speaking terms.

The next morning I'm planning to clear the air with him, but as soon as he walks in I see the sunken-eyed look of a Missoula winter. "It's the middle of winter. I'm broker than hell, without a prospect in sight," he says. And in Chaz's case, with one more baby and a wife with real problems.

Chaz tells me that winter should be the time to kick back and finish projects around the shop, get ahead with his bikes, but that instead he is busy scratching just to get by. He tells me he's stopped taking the Zoloft, because it has screwed him up somehow, left him without his hustling edge.

This is hard to listen to. It's entirely possible this medication saved my life, and I want to say, "Forget your damn 'hustling edge.' Go home and take a pill, Chaz."

If I order a set of fenders from him, it means a hundred bucks for Chaz, and for me it's a big leap ahead with the project. They *are* expensive—$750 or so—but I like the idea of having the fenders on the way, because it means whatever else happens, I will have all my sheet metal on hand and I'll be ready to paint.

"Hey, Chaz," I say. "I'll tell you what. If you can get them here in two weeks' time, go ahead and order those fenders for me."

Chaz is visibly cheered. "Good move," he says. "I'll get right on it."

The next day Chaz wants to sell me an older speedometer that will fit my dash perfectly.

"How much?" I ask.

"Are you interested or just curious?"

"Well, does it work?"

"Oh," says Chaz. "He wants one that *works,* too."

The truth is, a speedometer is about the last thing I'm concerned with right now, either working or nonworking. The dash and speedo are cosmetics to me, and Chaz seems not tuned in to this at all.

Later in the week, I call to see if he's connected with the fender maker and he tells me with annoyance that he hasn't come up with the number yet, grouses about how much he's spent on toll calls to try to get it.

"Whoa, but this was all *your* idea!"

He tries once more to sell me the broken speedo.

"Chaz," I tell him. "Why would I want that? How am I going to tell how fast I'm going if the thing is broken?"

With the very last of his patience he says, "By the sound of your damn motor, Fred!" and hangs up.

The end of Phoebe's first week home, the thaw begins. The town is awash in melting snow. At Phoebe's first checkup we find that in her week home she has lost nearly a pound. There's just not enough milk coming out, and poor Caroline is nearly in shock. She's fitted with a supplemental feeding system that involves a bottle worn around the neck and micro feeder tubes out to the breasts.

The floods continue and the hillside's turned to brown streaked with white, and I'm beginning to smell it now, the earth beneath the thawing ice. An ice jam breaks free up the Blackfoot, nearly takes out the Marcos Flats footbridge that hangs twelve feet above the water. Phoebe's color grows rosy with the supplement, and she continues to eat heartily.

By the river, a crowd of people stand by the footbridge while Search and Rescue looks for the body of a university student who either fell or jumped into the river. There's a big power shovel piling up ice. A couple of men with chain saws work on the slabs and pump out the slough. It's almost festive, and you can't help wondering, What the hell was that poor kid *thinking* when he was still alive last week?

I stop by the Carnal Garage to get a missing shackle for my fork. Chaz has stacked, hung, and arranged most of his parts, and you can actually walk through there now. It looks like things are happening—Chaz is building a 1950s Harley KR racer. Its stubby, bulletlike, mean-looking, and I think, Wow, when he wants to, Chaz can really do nice work!

I call Magoo to figure out our painting window, and I book in with him for the end of March. Then I call Chaz to advise him of that, and he tells me I won't make that, because he's already ordered the fenders with an eight-week delivery time,

"Eight weeks? I told you I needed them in *two*."

"Hey," says Chaz. "*You* were the one who told me to go ahead and order."

"I did not."

"Fred. You did. You're probably just having another one of your lapses."

"Goddammit, Chaz, I'm trying to stay on a schedule here. Why would I authorize an order that puts me six weeks behind? I'm planning to ride this bike this summer, not stare at it."

I hang up the phone in a state. Had I ordered them myself, I could have had the fenders here by now. With Chaz brokering the purchase, in three weeks' time we've exchanged a dozen phone calls and there are no fenders anywhere in sight. The only thing we've accomplished is that everyone's mad as hell. From now on I'll order my own damn parts.

More than a week passes before Chaz and I work in the trees again. It's a big silver maple, and the sun is shining, the sap is gushing from the cuts. The customer is an old hipster—cigarette-smoking, wisecracking. Such is the power of the day, it's as though none of the parts stuff had ever happened. Chaz says the cottonwood budding along the river is his favorite smell. Funny. I would have thought Chaz's favorite smell would be some seventy-year-old lithium-based wheel bearing grease out of a 1928 two-cam JD Harley.

He mentions that he's found another buyer for the fenders he ordered. I could have told him then that I've ordered my own fenders, but I don't want to risk it. I'm suddenly optimistic that we will get this thing together yet.

Chaz stops by on his way to the big swap meet in Portland. Without a trace of rancor, he admires my freshly mounted tires, the whitewalls bright and merry as Christmas ornaments, winking at us from the back of the garage. He is all excited about a one-ton Dodge dump truck he's been trying to buy for the past eight months, and it now appears he's closing on it. It's good to hear Chaz excited again. He says he's located a front cylinder for the Scout motor he's building, and if we can strike a deal for my 74-inch flywheels, he can stroke his 45ci Scout to 57ci.

"Jeez," I tell him. "I wish I could go along."

"Yeah," says Chaz. "It's too bad. Ken is sure to be there, and you guys could hang out together."

"Hang out together?"

"Yeah, sure. You could ask him all about your motor." He grins. "Maybe go off and smoke a doobie with him."

For the first time in months, Caroline gets to go out. I'm home alone with Phoebe, who wakes up after ninety minutes and begins to holler. I keep my head, make up a bottle of Nutramigen, and watch *NYPD Blue* while she takes it eagerly. It's the first time she's drunk straight formula, the first time she's even taken a bottle. She was miserable and now she's a delight, and I think, This changes everything. Caroline comes home a short time later to find Phoebe happily sucking away and is mildly shocked. While Caroline takes her off to bed, I look outside, watch the snow come down in big fluffy flakes. The cat sits at the window, the diaper bag sits on the front porch waiting for pickup, frozen solid, no doubt. Wow. It's a terrific life! But whatever happened to my motor?

I have coffee with Chaz after the Portland meet.

"Did you see Ken?"

"Yeah. I saw him. He's great. He was telling me how these Indian motors were made to be rebuilt over and over and over."

"That's sure good to hear. Did the subject of *my* motor come up?"

"No. I mean, not exactly."

Chaz tells me that he did happen to pick up a chromium kickstand, genuine Indian, while he was there. He looks at me pointedly. "I got it for *you*." He says this as if it were a gift, but if there's one thing I'm certain of, it's that it's not a gift.

"Well, do you want it?" he says.

"I dunno," I tell him. I'm afraid to ask how much he wants for it, because it's a question that, lately, seems to really set him off.

"Probably," I say, although I would prefer black to chrome. Once again, I get the feeling that if Chaz has anything to do with it, by the end of summer my Chief will look pretty much as it is now, without a front end or fenders, but with lots of spiffy accessories like chrome-plated kickstands and nonworking speedometers.

If I can get the front fork done, I can begin to put this Chief back together, but I'm avoiding it like crazy. What if I break something? What if I get it all apart and forget how it went together?

At Magoo's suggestion, to save us all time, I've jobbed the fork out to another welder and restorer named Rick Myers, a gray-bearded North End biker with a Knucklehead frame in his living room. I get it back in a couple of weeks and it looks terrific, but Rick points out that the upper part of the triple tree has a definite downward camber, which means it's either a unique Indian design feature that nobody ever noticed or that somebody bent it by banging into something.

I'm discouraged, because it means I've done things backward, and with the cosmetic work now completed, I have to get on with the fixing and rebuilding of this fork. What *is* it about the fork that has me so cowed? Maybe because it's so critical—the mechanism by which the rest of the bike is controlled. It's probably as simple as this: I've stared at it, handled it, flipped it all around, and I still haven't a clue how the girder-style fork works. But mostly, I'm daunted by the task of getting those old needle bearings out, and it seems like a good time to go see Chaz.

He's got his classics—the Scouts and the UL, VL, and WL Harleys—all lined up by year in the front of the garage. There is a sense of order that radiates out from that KH racer, taking shape over by the workbench. Behind us, in the driveway, sits Chaz's latest acquisition, a jonquil-yellow '74 Dodge dump truck. The hood is off it and the motor is in parts. Chaz'z friend Bummy, a biker and ex–long-haul trucker, is hard at work, replacing the head gasket and starter motor.

Chaz complains discreetly about how much it's costing him.

"Well, why don't you do that yourself?" I ask.

"Me?" says Chaz. "Hell, *I'm* no mechanic."

"Oh my God, Chaz," I tell him. "Don't say that about yourself. I *hate* it when you say that."

CHAPTER 11

MILLENNIUM BLUE

Over coffee, a carpenter named Brian tells me that in a recent *Easy Rider* magazine there's a feature on a Knucklehead Harley with a cedar frame and all-cedar fenders.

"For real?"

"Oh yeah—the December issue."

"Isn't that the Harley they called the 'Woodenhead'?" I suggest.

"No," says Chaz. "I believe they called it the 'Knothead.'"

We end up back at the Carnal Garage, where I drag in my box of fork parts and we sweep aside a place on the bench by the Harley KH. I was able to get one bearing race out by driving a flattened washer through, but these others were stuck fast, and we hunker down to have a look at three remaining bearings. Chaz whacks the top one out in pretty short order with an oversize punch, but the lower two require two sets of hands and two different punches, a blunt one and a sharp one. It is one of those very simple-looking jobs that end up taking a couple of hours, but throughout, I'm impressed by Chaz—his patience, his humor, and most of all, his touch.

This is the first time I've really seen him at work. I had him figured for a whacker, but after a lot of serious pounding, the freshly painted fork legs get off with a couple of very minor nicks, both of them inflicted by myself. We've just finished with the bearings when I spot the top of a Chief tree in a clutter of other parts and have a quick look at it. By eyeball, it's plain to see it's straighter than mine. I show Chaz the scoring on my shackle bolt.

"Yes. This has definitely been tweaked. Maybe someone going off a curb, hard to say, but the bolt was rubbing on the bend. Run out and grab us a can of hydraulic oil, Stroker. We'll straighten it right now on my metal press."

I pick up the oil, come back, and Chaz is on the phone. I'm hanging around the living room by the big woodstove when Yvonne comes in. For the first time since I've known her, she wears a bit of eyeliner, and the effect is dramatic. She's a very a striking woman. Yvonne scares me, and I'm not sure why. But I can tell that she knows this. And I think she likes it, too.

She heckles me good-naturedly about how long my project is taking, then she brings Aydyn downstairs. He's in a zebraskin sleeper and he's got a big round head and a grin like a jack-o-lantern.

"How's Phoebe doing?" says Yvonne.

"Okay," I tell her, but looking at Aydyn, there's not much of a comparison. Phoebe eats like a horse but stays tiny. Going on seven weeks, she's just over eight pounds and she's only twenty-three inches long.

"Don't worry about it," says Yvonne. "Some babies are just small. So what color are you going to paint your Chief?"

"What color do you think I should paint it?"

"I don't know," she says. "It's so personal. But it seems like all the Chiefs I've seen are either black or red."

I mention the robust midnight blue of Steve LaRance's Ford Victoria, and Yvonne lights up.

"Really," she says, "that would look just *awesome* on a Chief."

"Do you think? Chaz thinks it would look tacky."

Yvonne snorts. "Oh, Chaz doesn't like it? Have you looked at *his* bikes? His favorite color is rust!"

As if on cue, Chaz is back. He says, "Hey, you want to bend that treetop now?"

We unstack several layers of parts from his metal press, prime it with fluid, "tool up" with various shims to hold the tree in place, then place it on the anvil, bent side up. Chaz pulls on the handle, brings the ram down on it, stops, pulls on it some more. I wonder what it would cost to replace that tree if we snap it, but after a couple of attempts, we're able to pass the shackle bolt through it cleanly.

Yvonne comes out with with a load of laundry and says, "What are you guys doing *now?*"

"Oh," says Chaz. "We're trying to straighten out this piece of junk some asshole sold to Fred."

It's not a precision job, but the bolt shaft moves freely and it didn't before. It's a basic working-stiff shade-tree repair, and it's effective. More important, I'm losing my inhibitions about working on this bike. I'm learning to trust my eye and my common sense, and I'm beginning to understand that, like farm machinery, these old bikes were built for repairs exactly like this one, to be made by people not unlike myself.

The fork is now ready to rebuild and mount. I'm hugely encouraged by this burst of activity. It feels as if we've accomplished more than we have in months. I'm starting to believe this motorcycle can actually be done by summer.

Already Caroline's talking about play groups for Phoebe, and I'm not ready for that. Also, there's this business about exposing the child to

Mozart. I think of all the families that wouldn't dream of playing Mozart for their own enjoyment, but if it will make their baby a genius, it's worth it. It makes me grumpy. Next thing, we'll be reading her Faulkner and Camus, and she's not even two months old yet.

Phoebe and I spend the mornings together. She went through a week or two of crying spates, but she's much more her old self, doesn't fly into a rage when I change her. She's *very* strong in her legs and her neck, the way she holds her body rigid when she's mad, the way she pushes off my rib cage. I've discovered the bottle, and as of yesterday, there's Aydyn's old windup swing, which puts her to sleep in minutes. This morning I read my parts catalogues, then watch her sleep. I think back to my first baby, and I have to smile. Thirty years ago, I wouldn't change a diaper for God almighty.

Yvonne comes over with Aydyn. While the little babies stare at each other, she tells Caroline stories about their biker friends who drop in and just never leave.

"My God," I say. "It's like you're describing *me,* Yvonne."

She waves her hand. "Christ, no," she says. "I'm talking about people who show up out of nowhere and just *stay,* people who roll through on their way to Sturgis. Maybe their bike breaks down and they crash with us till their parts arrive. Then, of course, they have to use Chaz's shop to work on it."

The whole conversation makes me nervous, so I head over to the Carnal Garage, where I catch Chaz on his way to the dump with another load of stuff—a fifty-five-gallon drum, a sack of old muscle T-shirts, several defunct stereos. I help him tarp it up, realize there is something tidal about Chaz and his junk—the way a load comes in, a load goes out. Is his junk somehow in synch with the moon?

I buy him coffee at our afternoon spot, The Break, where I bump into the local artist, Rudy Autio. Rudy says he's heard I'm rebuilding an Indian Chief, and I feel like this is my chance.

"I am, Rudy," I say. "And I need your help. What color should I paint it?"

Without hesitation he says, "Oh, you must paint it *black*."

"Wow. Okay."

"And yellow," says Rudy. "And red, and blue, and, oh yeah, orange, too."

"I saw you talking to Autio," says Chaz when I return to our table.

"Yeah," I tell him. "I asked him what color to paint my bike."

"What'd he say?"

"I'm not sure. But I think he told me to paint it plaid."

The dog barks and the baby cries when UPS brings my fenders that night, and I pay out nearly the last of my Indian kitty for the COD. Hurriedly I rip open the huge boxes, haul the fenders out. They are enormous, bright, raw-looking, with all the spot welds, grinder marks, and rivets still visible. But even in this crude state they've got flowing, winglike lines. If only I could decide on the color!

The first day of spring, and Phoebe is upstairs in her Swyngomatic. She has a little pink hat pulled down to her eyes and she's listening to *Le Sacre du Printemps* on the radio—let's see all those Mozart freaks top that! I watch her and think of all the things that have changed this year, all the little ways that I've changed. I listen to lite rock on the radio (though that's mostly because the other stations are so crummy). I meet my friends for coffee instead of beers, and my Levi's waist size has crept from a thirty-four to a thirty-six.

Once Phoebe falls asleep, I call Magoo to tell him the fenders and chain guard have arrived and that I'm ready to bring them in for painting.

He's quiet for a moment, then he says "Well, have you got them all drilled out?"

"'Drilled out'?"

"Yes—the holes for your fender and taillights, for your trim strips, your cables, electrics, and mounting bolts. You'll want to get that all straightened out before you get your paint on there."

"I will?"

"Absolutely. You don't want to be running a high-speed drill around seven hundred dollars' worth of fresh paint, do you?"

I hang up the phone. I've allowed myself to think of this restoration as being in full stride, somehow in synch with the change in seasons. Now I see that to drill the fenders I first have to mount them, and to do that I need to reassemble my fork, so I have something to mount them *on*. And to do that, I need my steering dampener parts. I need to study more diagrams to see how that head goes on, and I need to finish doing whatever it was I'd decided to do to my rear springs—in short, to drill these fenders and get on with the paint will require another two weeks' work, at best.

The winds kick up again. Sunday morning I'm driving along Gerald, and there's a big spruce top hung in a maple by the Unity Church. I park the car, walk into the church, and find several board members, discussing what to do. I introduce myself, produce a card, give them a bid. They seem startled by the timing of it all; it's as if the Lord had sent me. For all I know, He did, but inside of an hour Chaz and I are on the job, and I'm going up what's left of that spruce. The wind comes right down the canyon, out of the east, which unfortunately is the only place to put that top. I notch it out, then hang there in my harness, timing the gusts, and when it's quiet for a moment, I quickly make the back cut. It's a big top, a twenty-five-footer, and on the way down, it sails dangerously toward the chimney but lands well short of it. The whole church board's turned out for this cut, and a ragged cheer erupts.

Later, on the way home, Chaz tells me how the treasurer told him she thought we had a "really good energy."

"No shit? We do?"

"Yeah." He turns to me, scowls, and says, "Are we going to let her get away with that?"

The next few days it blows too hard to climb. Phoebe still sleeps late, and I'm restless. I stalk around the house till I find myself in the garage. Something is wrong out here. It looks scattered and crowded. There's no room for the Chief.

I begin to move things around. I stow the barbecue, the skis, and bicyles against the far wall. I hang up all my ropes and climbing gear, put my chain saws under the bench, and in doing so, reclaim the whole rear of the garage. I back the Subaru up to the doors, load in a winter's worth of recycling, and the whole garage has opened.

I look at my watch. It didn't even take an hour. Why didn't I do this last month? I fix on Chaz's old Ford differential—the shade-tree cycle stand he loaned me, propped against the rear wall. I drag it forward, dust it off, set it on the concrete beneath the hanging lightbulb. I place the little turntable on the top and spin it around. Suddenly I'm drilling deep holes in the concrete floor with a masonry bit, bolting the stand down with expansion bolts. I spin the table again. *Solid!* I hoist the frame on, arrange a pair of brackets, pad the frame with carpet remnants, and bolt it securely to the top of the turntable. *Terrific!* The stand holds my Chief about four feet high, so I can work on it standing up or sitting down. It rotates completely, so I can get at it from any side. Next I hang the primered gas tanks on and spin the table again. This is a watershed moment, and I can't get enough of it. I keep closing the doors, then opening them again, just to see it: the true beginnings of a motorcycle. In the space of the baby's nap time, the Chief is up off the floor. My work space is transformed from a garage to a *shop,* and though I will have to take them off again, with the bolting on of the gas tanks, the reassembling has begun.

I'm back in the house flushed with success, and Phoebe is still asleep! There is a brief message on the phone from my agent. She says it's too soon to tell, but that maybe I've finally sold my novel. Then again, maybe I haven't.

The pussy willows I brought home a couple months back are finally starting to sprout, but it's suddenly very cold and it seems spring is in retreat. It's getting to everyone. Particularly, I think it's getting to Chaz. I called him up last night to thank him for the loan of the bike stand, to tell him how well it works, and immediately he cops an attitude: How'd you mount it? What kind of bolts did you use? Where'd you get the drill bit?

He's firing questions at me like a cop, and I realize I've screwed up, crossed him again, but I don't even know where. Should I have asked him to help me set it up? I haven't a clue.

He brings Bummy by my shop after work and we sit around, gape at the Chief on its stand. There is more talk about paint jobs. In a rant against Millennium Blue, Chaz is at his most eloquent yet. He says there is nothing in the world that looks worse than a vintage motorcycle rendered in "some cheesy-ass color."

"Fred," he says. "You *know* that black is going to look terrific. It's going to look dynamite. But the blue? I mean, who can say?"

"It looks good on LaRance's Ford."

Chaz looks pained. "Sure," he says. "But that's a *car*."

———

The weather stays bad. But with the long winter over and spring on the way, the view from my shop is like this:

Tanks rebuilt, primed
Frame repaired, straightened, painted
Wheels rebuilt, laced, and trued
Tires mounted and balanced
Brakes rebuilt
Fork painted
Sheet-metal work in progress

It's not a bad winter's work, and with the arrival of my shackle bushings and steering-dampener wheel, I'm ready to start putting this big motorcycle together. But before I do anything, I need to figure out where the mounting holes go on my fenders.

I walk a couple blocks north and stop at Craig Eddy's place. Craig is in the driveway, replacing the fuel pump on his grandma's '53 Packard Clipper. He's jovial as always, invites me in to take my measurements on that front fender. But with the Chief's head fender light, the curvature and all the angles, it is really hard to do. I stay a half hour, make some terribly crude measurements, and decide I've had enough for today. But before I leave I say, "You're a man of the world, right, Craig?"

"There's a case to be made for that."

"You're a man of taste and refinement, right?"

Craig grins. "There's a case to be made for that, too."

"I was thinking of painting my Chief midnight blue. What do you think?"

Craig pauses for a moment. "Hey, man," he says. "I mean, your numbers don't match. Your bike's going to be cobbled together out of a bunch of parts anyway, right? Go ahead and paint it whatever the hell color you like."

I'm stung by that one. Craig has just dismissed my project as if I'm building some clownmobile. I guess that's why I go and get drunk over at Peter Stark's that night. That and the phone call I get from my dad, who has the bad taste to bewail the fact that we're all so far apart.

Peter starts in on the subject of his own family; I rattle on about mine. It's all pretty boring, but the booze has started to flow. Finally Peter says, "Fred—what can you expect? We're krauts, you and me. We come from kraut families. It's a known fact that kraut families lay more screwball trips on their kids than any other ethnicity could ever dream of."

At the time this is the most brilliant thing I've ever heard, and I leave Peter's feeling curiously at peace with the question of Pop. It makes his distancing, aloofness, cruelty, and cynicism less a personality trait, more a cultural phenomenon.

I wait for more parts, and in the meantime pin the rear fender to the frame with two mounting tab bolts and a big C-clamp. I can't get enough of the way it looks, which is like a fuselage part from a 1940s Lockheed Vega. Something inside of me begins to kick over at the sight of it—this machine looks like it's in flight. And after a long and turbulent winter, my garage suddenly feels like a place where something is about to happen.

CHAPTER 12

A CYCLONE IN A JUNKYARD

ONE MORNING IN EARLY SPRING, I OPEN MY GARAGE DOORS AND there—in the midst of the yard tools, mowers, snow tires, steer manure, Miller bottles, and newspapers—back there in the gloom, on a single graceful pedestal, a fabulous machine has been taking shape in the darkness.

I see this bike rising from behind the recycling and I'm reminded of the creationist's hedge against the Big Bang theory—that human life is so intricate, complex, and miraculous, it's no more likely to have arisen from a single blast of energy than a 747 could come to being from a cyclone in a junkyard. There must be some larger intelligence at work behind the scenes. But who's the larger intelligence in this garage?

In April, Sara flies out to see her baby sister. When I pick her up, I say, "Well, Sara, what would you like to do now that you're here? We could go check out the Unabomber arraignment in Helena or we could drive over to Jordan and see how the Freemen standoff is going."

It's a joke, of course, but like many of my friends, I take a kind of perverse pride in Montana's unique brand of celebrity, just because, when you live in a state with 800,000 people, how often do you get to hear the CNN anchor say, "Elsewhere in Montana today . . ."?

In the end, the four of us drive to Big Sky for a weekend of skiing. Caroline has broken her foot in a freakish fall on the sidewalk. She's still in a cast, and she's grumpy about it all. She should be—the skiing is *terrific*.

Sara and I ride the new tram clear to the top. At 12,000 feet or so, the skiing is Double Diamond, and neither of us feels much like skiing this peak. Maybe that's just because we're about the only skiers in the tram who aren't wearing helmets.

We finish the day with some beers at the Cinnamon Bear down the Gallatin River. Sara asks me my feelings about tattoos. Am *I* planning to get one?

I tell her I don't know yet.

She tells me she and Kyle have had tattoos for a while. I'm mildly shocked. I press her for details about Kyle, which she seems happy to relate. Kyle is pulling it together. He finished the last three credits he needed, received his B.A., got a job with a software outfit in the city. Now, if only Sara can get him fixed up with the right girlfriend.

Even an absentee parent understands there's always the possibility they're telling you what they think you want to hear, but I don't care. I'm happy just to have this time with her. Mostly because I understand that, even after the years of recriminations between her stepfather and me, Sara and I have what we have today simply because we wouldn't give up on it. I'm feeling more comfortable with Sara then I ever have before. I'm even comfortable enough to try to tell her why I left.

"The marriage was a burning house, Sara. It was the only way we could all survive. I don't believe your mom's a bad person, I don't believe that I'm a bad person, either. Your mom and I just had a knack for bringing out the worst in each other."

It was my big chance to explain myself—why I did what I did. I must have rehearsed this little speech a thousand times in twenty-five years. But having finally delivered it, it sounds thin, simplistic, and I end up feeling deflated and anxious. I wonder if my little summary is enough. If it could *ever* be enough.

Sara sits quietly, seems to digest this for a moment. Her eyes are sad, and she says, "Yes. I had a relationship like that once, too." Then she excuses herself, heads to the women's room. I watch, fascinated, as an old cowboy down the bar hits on her, and then I see her brilliant smile, hear her say, "You better watch yourself, mister —" and she points over to me. "See that big guy at the end of the bar? That's my *father*."

Back in Missoula, around nine o'clock, Sara looks up at the inky blue-black sky and says, "Is *that* it? Millennium Blue? The color blue you're going to paint the Indian?"

My heart leaps. "Yes," I tell her. "*Exactly* like that, Sara." It all seems so auspicious, and yet it doesn't end there, because when we get home I find my parts shipment, including the missing steering head bearings, stuck inside my front door, waiting for me.

It's eighty degrees, and nobody's ready for that. It seems unfair—we never even had a chance to start thinking about shorts, and suddenly summer is here.

I put Sara on the seven A.M. red-eye, come home, and fall asleep with Phoebe for a couple of hours. In the afternoon I drive to East Missoula to prune a willow. Chaz and Bummy bring the rebuilt Dodge, and we make an afternoon of it. The job features a crotchety old man, a poodle named Mickey, and more brush than I've seen in a while, but the whole time I'm working that tree, I think about the Chief's steering head. It's been lying around my house for a week while I try to figure out which side is up for the splash washers—and the bearings themselves, for that matter. The steering dampener sounds gritty inside, but the diagram looks so complex with its stack of washers, gaskets, and bearings, I'd do almost anything to avoid taking it apart.

Chaz and Bummy come by my shop after work. Chaz takes a look at my new bearings and guffaws. "Har har. What'd they ding you for *these?* Only twice what they're worth, or three times?" He holds the box up to the light, pretends to read: "Made *where*? 'People's Republic of China'? Hoo-ha!"

In fact, they were made in France, but it feels terrible, this ragging, even when we determine the upper set of bearings were made in the United States. But the worst part is when he tells me I could have bought these same parts for peanuts down at the local bearings shop.

Humiliated and chastened, I follow Chaz's advice and drive to the bearings shop, where I discover that the same set of bearings I paid $24 for would cost $50—on back order. I return to my garage with my self-respect intact.

I tap the retrofit bushings into the shackle holes with a drift punch, then move on quickly to the steering head. I get the lower bearing in place, but the upper race is exactly an eighth of an inch too wide and there's no getting around it. There follow about half a dozen long-distance discussions about what the problem could be, and finally the man at Rocky's, where I bought them, is stumped. "They're too *wide?* Boy. Is that ever weird. Well, send 'em on back."

It's not until Chaz comes by the next morning that I realize the old race is still in place—that I was trying to fit the new race on top of it. In the eight months I've worked on this bike, this is the dumbest I've felt to date. Chaz and I pop the old race out with a punch just as Caroline hands Phoebe off on her way to work, and it becomes Phoebe's first morning in the garage. While Chaz and I finish the steering head, she takes a bottle, naps on the old pickup seat.

We break for coffee and Chaz fixes on the chrome kickstand he brought back from Seattle weeks before, which is now lying on a shelf.

"I can't believe you pissed all over this stand, after all I went through to get it." He shakes his head. "Aww. Maybe I just ought to sell it to someone else."

"You mean somebody who could appreciate it?"

"Yeah," he says. "Someone like that."

The Chief battery tray is an integral part of the rear fender mount. My tray is rusted, partly eaten away by battery acid, so I take it to Ronnie the Welder's to get it rebuilt.

Ronnie's shop is a couple miles past East Missoula and consists of two war-surplus Quonset huts placed end to end. It begins to storm while I'm there, and the hailstones on the corrugated steel are deafening. Ronnie's yard is full of derelict vehicles, lots of 1950s Willys "Overland" wagons.

Ronnie is a vital, exuberant young man with inexhaustible energy. His shop is impressive—brightly lit, orderly, well equipped. The yellow minisubmarine out front is Ronnie's own handiwork, and he loves to tell about its first voyage to the bottom of Flathead Lake. I leave Ronnie so he can reinforce the bottom of the tray and then restore the battery retainer lip. I return home where, once more, I attempt to mount the fork on the steering head—all of this so I can hang the front fender and map where the mounting holes should be. But ninety minutes later I'm defeated again, and I quit before I break something.

The next morning I collar Chaz, tell him that I'm stumped.

"Truth is," he says, "those shackles are kind of a four-handed project."

"Tell you what, Chaz. It's worth a hundred bucks to get your two hands in on this. I want to get those fenders over to Magoo's, and the sooner the better."

Instantly we are back in my shop and parts are flying. We're moving along briskly for the first hour, until we realize one of the shackle-bolt rods is bent. We run back to Chaz's metal press, straighten the bolt out in a hailstorm, then head out to East Missoula to pick up my battery tray. There is so much coffee involved in these errands that by the time we get to Ronnie's shop, we're traveling at warp speed, nearly exhausted.

Chaz turns to me and sighs. "Ahh, this is *way* too much work, Stroker. Why don't you just trade me your half-baked Indian pile for a good-running Shovelhead?"

Magoo himself comes over to check my progress. He admires the reproduction fenders, says they will be easier to work on than original sheet metal. After fifty-some years, those are generally so full of rust, holes, and body putty that they might take weeks to prep.

We're on the floor, Magoo and I, rolling around on the cat litter I've scattered over the oil spills, trying to clamp the front fender on the fork. The halogen light is blazing overhead, and to my astonishment I discover mounting-bolt holes are prescribed in the metal. It's so faint, you can barely see it without the powerful light, but when I check the rear fender, the same is true there—all except for the lateral mounting bolts. I ask Magoo why they would scribe all the holes but those, and he says it's because there's so much variation on the way those parts fit from machine to machine. "With those particular holes, it's every man for himself."

The scribings are a revelation. They save us hours of measurements and eyeballing. Still, the holes for the accessories—like trim strips, rear bumper and luggage rack—are not accounted for, and Magoo tells me I need to order these parts, mock them up, and drill them out before we go on to the painting. He watches my face fall at the prospect of another week's delay, and he says, "Hey, don't worry about it. You're still moving along about twice as fast as most people."

I know this, but somehow I'm still in a race. There have been dozens of delays to this point, and if there's one thing that's certain, there will be dozens more.

That night at a party I see my old writing guru Bill Kittredge, and he says, "I hear you sold your novel, Fred."

"That's funny, Bill," I tell him. "I've heard that too." The truth is, since I heard the month before that two small presses were interested, I've had no word whatsoever. I'm thinking about how a year ago this would have driven me right up the wall. A year ago I would have been beside myself. But now I've got bigger things to worry about. Now I've got an Indian.

CHAPTER 13

BURNING HOUSES

THERE'S A HUGE CHLORINE SPILL THIRTY MILES TO THE WEST. The whole town of Alberton's evacuated and living in motels out on the Missoula franchise strip, and the interstate's closed "indefinitely." I've seen nothing like this since Mount Saint Helens blew up sixteen years ago.

Chaz is down. He's fighting with Yvonne again, whom he's taken to calling "the War Department." It has to do with the kids, with the way she spends her time, and, of course, with money. Also, something about a new medication she's taking that has peculiar side effects.

"It's not supposed to," he says grimly. "But you can tell it just really kicks her ass."

One half of me wants to listen closely, so I can offer suggestions. The other half of me wants to not hear any of it, because I don't feel there *are* any helpful suggestions. I feel like I know this situation backward and forward. It's the old Burning House.

We end up looking at our progress on the Chief, and it distracts him. In a short time, he's feeling better enough to ask me if I want to buy in on a 1952 Ford he's been eyeballing. We can get it cheap, he says. We can turn it around for twice what we pay at the big hot-rod show this weekend.

"Look, Chaz," I tell him. "By now you should know I don't *have* thousand-dollar bills lying around my house. I've got just about enough money left for my paint job."

Chaz snorts. "Shit, man. You could *double* that eight hundred by this weekend, if you only had the heart to buy in."

Ronnie comes by to see how badly my chain guard doesn't fit, and he's not disappointed: It doesn't fit at all. He takes several measurements, draws a couple sketches, and says that if he grinds the back side off, fills in on the lower edge, drops the lower mounting bracket a quarter inch, then whacks a quarter inch off the left front corner of the rear fender, maybe it will fit.

I quote Magoo, who says if you can get Indian sheet metal to touch in three out of four places, you're well ahead of the game. I tell him, "Ronnie, I'm in your hands."

How many times I've told people that in the last year! I watch him pack my chain guard and rear fender into his pickup, and head back to grind, torch, splice, and braze my chain guard into shape. I marvel over the welder's art, which is to change what would seem to be the unchangeable.

Ronnie's straightened out my brake and clutch pedals, both of them badly bent in some cycle wreck long ago. He explains how he'd broken both pedals in the straightening, but the new welds will be stronger than the original steel. They are so subtle, you can barely see them, and he's cleaned all the rust away on his grinder wheel. He tells me that while he was working on them, some old boy comes in to get a quick weld, spots my pedals, and immediately starts talking Indian. The man told him the heel and toe pads affixed to my clutch pedal were off a Harley, that they would not work on an Indian.

"So," I tell Ronnie. "You mix your clutch-pedal pads and you burst into flames?" I'm beginning to really like the sound of this.

Ronnie grins. "*I* don't know. That's just what he said."

As if on cue, a burly-looking old fellow in a bow hunter's cap strides into the shop and greets Ronnie.

"Fred," says Ronnie. "Here he is: Meet Bob Hardy."

Bob looks hale and tough, appears to be in his late sixties. He says he comes from Syracuse, that at one time he had seventeen Indians in his garage.

"But," he says, "then I had to raise a bunch of kids."

"What happened to the bikes?"

He shakes his head. "Had to get rid of 'em. They were eating my life." He gestures to my clutch pedal, the one with the Harley heel and toe pads. "Those won't work on an Indian," he says flatly.

I'm tantalized by this piece of information. It seems like some ancient biker's goof, but Bob's expression is absolutely deadpan.

"So I leave these on, I'll miss all my shifts?"

Bob shrugs. "They just won't work."

I'm mystified, feeling gullible. Christ, it's just a pedal, not a wrist pin. How could it not work?

But Bob's moved on to an outpouring of Indian arcana that very shortly leaves me in the dust: the differences in the primary cases, valve-cover differences between the '41 and '47 motors, etc. He tells me that Indians were just "always naturally faster than Harleys." Bob studies me a moment to see if I'm getting all this.

"Hey," he says. "You're restoring a Chief? I got a guy for you to call. Name is Charles Darling and he lives upstate New York. He's got a garage full of Indian parts. Call him up and tell him old Bob Hardy sent you. Tell him it's the guy who sold him the Henderson motor back there in 1972."

When I get home, I call Chaz, tell him I met a guy who had seventeen Indians at one time.

Chaz is silent for a moment. "Seventeen, huh?"

"Yeah."

"Sounds like he's full of shit, Fred."

"Well. Maybe it was sixteen, then."

I call Pop and tell him that Sara was just out to see her baby sister, and Pop falls silent for a moment. Then he complains bitterly of his estrangement from Sara, which sends me into a snit.

"You want to know why you're estranged? Okay, I'll tell you: Sara tried to visit you years ago and you blew it off. You told her you were too busy. You never tried to reschedule. You never sent a graduation present. You never even sent a birthday card, but most of all, you never sent a plane ticket. So you can't really blame Sara if you don't feel like you're very close."

"But, Fred," my father says. "I called her on the phone."

At issue is what I've come to know as Minimum Dad, my father's basic arm's-length policy. In the five months Phoebe's been around, there has been no card, gift, or move to see her. But he did call once, to see if she'd arrived safely.

Maybe it's unfair to feel this way and maybe it isn't, but I've come to see this as my father's towering indifference to anything beyond his own very fixed boundaries. I think of the way he threw up his hands at the airplane project long ago. "I'm just no good at these things," he said.

Did he mean me, too?

Tonight in my garage, the rear springs seem magically to go together. Tonight, for some reason, everything seems to fit better. In addition to aptitude, common sense, and good instincts, I guess a restorer also needs the right moon, too.

I bang the new rear spring covers on with my rubber mallet, compress the springs, and reinstall them in the frame. With these springs on and the fenders in place, I'm beginning to feel the full gravitational pull of this project—how big and powerful the bike is beginning to look, with its great sprung chest and smallish hindquarters.

It's nearly midnight, and I'm still out here ogling it when Caroline comes to the door and says in a very grumpy voice, "What do you *do* out here all this time?"

"I'm building me a motorcycle. What the hell you think?"

Phoebe's discovered her hands. She grabs things now, grabs the bottle, grabs my shirt. She grabs my face and then she won't let go. She's got my face in her hands when I hear on NPR that back east, this is the summer of the seventeen-year locust, the cicada. A seventeen-year cycle! The next time those creatures hatch, Phoebe will graduate from high school and I'll be looking at seventy.

She's still got ahold of my face when my agent Frankie calls to tell me that, four years later, I've finally sold my novel.

"My God," I tell her. "Are you sure?"

"Well, of *course* I'm sure," she says. "Really, I thought you'd be a bit more excited than this."

I hang up the phone, walk around awhile, cry, "Yes! Yes!" till I frighten the baby, but after four years it is slightly anticlimactic. Still. If the springs come together, if I've sold my novel, well, just *maybe* my motor is finished, too.

I call up Ken, who says, "Funny you should call. Your motor's all apart on my bench right this minute."

I whoop and cheer. Ken just chuckles.

Finally my sheet metal is fitted and all drilled out. I pile it in the back of my Subaru and head for East Missoula. Magoo thinks it looks pretty good, except maybe for the fender ornament holes, which are about a half inch too high. But I drop it all off, along with the formula for LaRance's midnight blue and an $80 deposit. I see the other Chief frame in there, and it looks like it's finally been straightened and touched up.

"Uh-oh," I tell Magoo. "He's gaining on me."

CHAPTER 14

INDIAN JOE

IT'S A SATURDAY AND THERE'S THREE OF US, CHAZ AND BUMMY and I, heading down I-90 eastbound for Butte, where there may or may not be a basketcase Indian, which may or may not be for sale. I'm prepared to buy in on this, and in my pocket is $500. I had to hijack this money from my paint job fund, but Chaz has finally talked me into it. In the back of the van are a variety of Harley Sportster parts, which, like blankets and beads, are available for barter if it should come to that.

We're all amped up on Coca-Cola, telling each other stories most of which begin with the line "Back when I was drinking . . ."

At first we take turns with this, but eventually Bummy, the ex-long-haul trucker, embarks on a running monologue.

"See right over there, by the bridge? One time I smoked a bowl when my Panhead took a dump. Over there by that curve? I traveled half a mile sideways with a forty-foot trailer, wall-to-wall black ice. Oh yeah—and over there, by those cottonwoods? I blew lunch there after my buddy slipped me an Olympia beer—I can't *stand* Olympia beer."

Finally Chaz says, "Damn, Bummy. You know, driving with you is a lot like traveling with Lewis and Clark: Over there we dumped a canoe. Over here I stepped in bear shit once."

We keep climbing into the Rockies, and at 5,700 feet we roll off the interstate among the wind-scoured brick buildings and decimated landscape that is Butte, Montana, where, a road sign announces, "it's a mile high, the mines are a mile deep, and all the people are on the level."

We stop at a pleasant, well-kept house on Massachusetts Avenue to pick up our connection, Manny Madrid. Like most of us, Manny is in his middle years. He's short and powerful-looking with a thick black beard, spectacles, and what looks like a triple E–size logger boot.

He scrambles into Chaz's van with the rest of us. We're on our way to Walkerville, a little township adjoining Butte, and on the way, Manny starts ragging on Chaz's van.

"Jesus, you really think we'll pull that hill in this hunk of shit? I dunno, Chaz . . . Hey, how are the brakes on this thing, anyway?"

After a couple minutes of this, Chaz is starting to get rattled. We try to gather speed for the Walkerville Hill. It seems as if we go almost vertically, and Chaz's van is literally gasping along when we finally level off. It *feels* high in Walkerville. It's windblown, exposed, markedly colder than Butte. We're surrounded by a cordon of peaks, and the century-old buildings seem to lean one against the other for support, hang out over thin air.

The biker we're looking for, known as "Big Cal," has run afoul of the law and bivouacs in a glass-brick storefront next to a bar called Pisser's Palace. I'm thinking I may have seen a rougher-looking bar than Pisser's, but I sure can't remember where. There's plywood thrown over the windows of Big Cal's place, and as we pull in Manny says, "Honk your horn, Chaz. Slam all the doors, talk really loud, and anything else you can think of. This guy's a little spooked, so you'll want to give him plenty of warning."

Bummy and I pile out, too. We're standing in front of the storefront while Manny tries to decide whether or not to knock on the door. Everyone's getting spooked.

Bummy turns to me and says, "What do you think? Will a .357 travel through a glass-brick wall?"

There is more hesitation, and finally Manny decides to go in the rear entrance, so Bummy and I head toward Pisser's Palace for a beer and a pee.

"Hey," says Manny. "You guys aren't thinking of goin' in Pisser's?"

Bummy and I look at each other. "Yeah," we say. "Sure."

"Well," says Manny. "Jesus Christ. Just . . . try not to act like tourists in there."

Pisser's is a low-ceilinged, windowless, concrete structure that resembles a blockhouse. There's a small knot of customers, watching the Team USA women's gymnastic finals. Bummy and I order a couple Millers, walk back outside with them. The men at the bar never even look up.

Back on the street, we see the storefront we were tiptoeing around is now open, and Bummy and I look at each other, shrug, and walk in.

The place is cold, damp, and dim, scarcely more habitable than your average cave. The walls are wood-grain vinyl, the floor is concrete, and aside from the sleeping bag wadded up in the corner, there is not much in the place that would suggest a human being was living there. There is most of a Shovelhead, most of a Sportster, and a couple of Indian piles. Standing barefoot in the midst of it all is a great hulking man in jeans and a T-shirt. He has hair down to his buttocks, and his beard is shot with bolts of silver. He is unsteady and can't seem to bring us into focus. He is either the most hungover individual I have ever seen or he has suffered some kind of concussion. Possibly both.

With the appearance of Bummy and me, Chaz performs the introductions with an exaggerated cordiality. We all shake hands, and Big Cal mumbles something in a register so low it might be some kind of seismic temblor. Whether this is an affable sound or a warning is impossible to say, but I'm aware we're all moving very carefully here.

Chaz suggests that as a potential investor I check out the Chief pile, and I do. The frame appears sound, not rusted out or torched up. The girder-style fork indicates it is a postwar vintage, '46 to '48. The chassis comes with both pedals and, unlike my own, with a kicker, too, which I immediately covet. There is a front and rear wheel and a set of tanks that are completely rotted through. Even through the grease, you can tell that the engine cases have been chromed. But when I kneel to check the serial number I find it's been completely effaced. In its place there is only the inscription "INDIAN JOE."

Chaz offers $2,500, but Big Cal shakes his head. Rather astonishingly, he's not as desperate as it might appear, and he draws himself up. "I've had this Chief for twenty years," he says with dignity. "It's, like, a part of my family, man."

On the way down from Walkerville, Manny and Chaz and Bummy are swapping yarns, but mostly I'm thinking about Big Cal's cave, how it's funny that places like that—sites of misery, chaos, and desperation—appear to be a natural habitat for these old motorcycles.

Meanwhile, Chaz tries to sell Manny a 96ci Evolution motor for $3,200.

"Naah," says Manny. "A guy was selling those in Helena last month for twenty-nine hundred."

That night, Chaz calls me on his cell phone to apprise me of the latest developments. I can tell it's the cell phone because, when you're not being shunted around to dispatches from the police or Fish and Wildlife bands, or bombarded with urgent Morse code dispatched from Lubumbashi, the phone hisses, spits, and pules like some skewered demon—though I happen to know he got a hell of a good deal on it.

Chaz tells me he made Big Cal another offer, $4,700 for the Indian *and* the Sportster basket, "with a few Harley parts thrown in."

"So did he bite?"

"He's going to think about it," says Chaz.

"So where'd you come up with the extra two grand?"

Chaz chuckles mysteriously. "From my backers, Stroker. From my backers."

On Monday, Chaz, Bummy, and I take down an eighty-foot Engelmann spruce behind Charlie Brookes's house, a couple blocks away. We arrive on the job, and before we get started, Charlie, a retired M.D., insists we pose before the tree for a group photo, "so we can see how many of you are left when this is over," he says with a grin.

We gear up, and I've just begun to climb when his wife, Helen, calls out to me, "And if you see that squirrel up there, *kill* it."

In case I haven't mentioned it, I have a phobic reaction to these tree-born rats, and I freeze for a moment. "Squirrels? What squirrels?"

Below me, I can hear Chaz do his best Royal Dano as he croaks, "Are ye *schared,* boy?"

It's gusty, but I keep working my way up, cutting off the limbs, and by the time I've reached the last ten feet it's quiet enough to free-fall the top. The spruce is roughly the height of an eight-story building, and when I finally stop for a break I realize there are a dozen or more people down there—old bulls, relatives, and various neighbors, sprawled in lawn chairs, drinks and cameras in their hands. I can tell they are impressed. I don't think anybody thought I'd get this far today. I know *I* certainly didn't.

The top sails down neatly and the party begins to disband. By the time I've worked my way back down the spar, they are all gone but Charlie, who pounds me on the back, brings me into his house, and pours me a glass full of Tullamore Dew. Charlie is practically blind, so he has me make out the check to myself.

"Hey, *sip* that stuff. Don't gulp it," he says. "Now, did you get it all made out the way you want it?"

"Yessir."

"Okay, now I'll sign it. . . . Is this where I sign it?"

"Yessir."

"Are you sipping that whiskey? You're supposed to sip it, you know."

Glug. "Yessir."

Chaz calls late that night to tell me Big Cal has accepted his offer. "*Now* what do I do?" he says.

"What do you mean? I thought this is what you wanted."

"Well—Indian Joe's already as good as sold, and that leaves me with another damn Sportster. I don't *want* another damn Sportster."

"Well," I tell him. "You *do* get to keep your Bonneville Chief now."

He sighs. "Yeah. Yeah, but I wanted to keep 'em both."

How *black* my Chief looked last night. The sheet metal is all fitted and off to Magoo's, and it's just that frame again. Caroline says it looks like a petroglyph up there on its stand, and I shine it, polish it, then polish it some more, as if I could bring it to life that way. I've mounted the fork, bolted on footboards and pedals, and once again I have an inkling of how big and powerful it is going to be.

I'm working only afternoons now, but I'm still getting beat up from the climbing. I end up with a physical therapist named Tim who says I should "get right on it," deal with these shoulders before they get too messed up to work with. He tells me I need to strengthen them with a series of strenuous exercises.

"Are you kidding?" I ask him. "I thought that was the problem."

I remain skeptical of him until I see the Harley-Davidson calendar on the wall. I ask if he is a rider and he says he is, though he got to it a little later in life.

"You and me both," I tell him.

And lying there on his examination table, Tim manipulates my shoulder, recounts how the first bike he had he bought from "a guy in East Missoula they called Parts Father."

When I get home there are four or five messages on the machine, and they're all from Chaz. They're all made on his satanic cellular phone. Chaz is on his way to Butte, and as he gets farther away, the calls get fainter and fainter, till on the last one he says wistfully, barely audibly:

"I really wish you were coming along, man. I'm afraid that bearded son of a bitch is going to shoot me in the head and take my money."

Yvonne drives by later that evening with a present—a tiny pink bunny for Phoebe. It seems she drove all the way over to deliver this, then she's gone in an instant. For some reason, she is bashful as some woods creature, even vulnerable, and it's odd, the way Yvonne sometimes seems so slight, even fragile—this hard-nosed, bartending, black-leather-wearing young woman. It's easy to see how Chaz could fall for her.

CHAPTER 15

TWENTY YEARS OF PAIN

THIS MAY THE FLAT-TRACK RACES ARE RAINED OUT BUT THE BIG Vintage Swap Meet goes on as planned, and as I cruise vendors and motorcycle wares, I think of how alien all this felt last year, not to mention threatening. But this year there are familiar faces everywhere, some of them people I've worked with, some of them friends: Manny and Bummy, Ronnie, Magoo, and Artie. Yvonne is working the gate, and I try to pay admission, but she brushes my money aside and stamps my hand.

Chaz is at his moving-and-shaking best. He zips around the booths, buying, selling, trading. I'm standing at Magoo's booth, talking to him, when a kid with a bum leg hobbles over and, without preamble, yanks up his shirt to display a tribal-style tattoo in the small of his back. Nobody is quite sure what this means, but it turns out the kid wants to know if Magoo can paint his Sportster tank with the same design.

Magoo studies the tattoo a moment. "Blue or black?" he asks.

Artie tries hard to sell me a set of Chief springs he's fabricated for fifty bucks. I tell him I probably would buy them if I hadn't already put my plungers back together and stuck them in the frame.

Artie shrugs. "Buy them anyway."

"It's too big a deal getting them all apart again."

"No, it's not," says Artie.

"It is for *me,*" I tell him.

I walk through the concourse where the enthusiasts display their bikes. Tom Benson, whom I met at Sturgis, has a pair of Indians on exhibit—a '37 Chief and a 1940 Scout Junior—and they are fine restorations with first-class paint jobs. The chrome is flawless, the fasteners look correct. There is a '60s Bonneville Triumph, a shiny BSA Thunderbolt, and at the end of this line is Chaz's Sport Scout, which remains rough as he bought it, except for the Harley exhaust pipe coming straight up off the header at a right angle, held in place with plumber's strapping. In this elegant line of restorations, Chaz's Scout looks funky. Clownish. *Beat.*

Aside from Willa's Mustang scooter, which isn't really a scooter and may not even be Willa's, I'm struck by the fact that Chaz doesn't have a restoration of his own. I've come to the conclusion that Chaz just likes them rough. He seems prouder of the derelict Indian Joe (which was not sold after all), which he displays bolted loosely together, much as my own Chief was. Still, Joe is getting as much attention as any bike in the place, and I understand that Chaz's peculiar genius is in presentation: the way he can "paint" the project in all its rough-hewn splendor. He paints it with words, he paints it with parts. It's the possibilities that move Chaz, not the fact.

It rains and floods through the month. Caroline and I go out to Big Flat for a hike, but the trails are washed out. All anybody wants to do is sleep, as the month turns into an endless, soggy blur. Phoebe wrestles her teddy bear. She grunts, chews it, slings it around like a Saturday-night wrestler. I toss her into the air, and she belly-laughs. She tries hard to talk—screws up her face, makes these marvelous guttural sounds. I wonder if somewhere down the line, in thirty years or so, Phoebe will feel the need to rebuild a 1997 Fat Bob Harley to ride back to Montana and explore her roots.

Once again, I'm waiting for parts. I've gone as far as I can with the chassis, and Magoo has my sheet metal. Ken, to the best of my knowledge, still has my motor, so it's time to get on with the business of trying to register an untitled bike.

I have every reason to believe this will be a complex and time-consuming process, but it's remarkably easy. The woman at DMV tells me all I need is my bill of sale and a police officer to "witness" the bike's serial number. She hands me a very short form for him to sign, and I call up Chaz for advice.

Chaz gives me a phone number off the top of his head, tells me Tim Monzon is a highway patrolman and biker.

When Monzon comes by, he brings another biker, the one they call Mort, to check out the restoration, and while Tim witnesses and signs off the form, Mort tells me about the '37 Chief he and a friend put together a few years back.

"Who was that?" I say.

"A guy they called Parts Father," says Mort.

I keep thinking that Tim looks familiar. I keep trying to place him, and then finally I do: He was the guy at the annual Montana Legends New Year's Ride—the one in the shemagh, the fez, and the riding breeches.

I'm back at the DMV in half an hour and the woman at registration peers at the form owlishly and says, "Indian? Never heard of an Indian. What's the color? You *are* going to paint it black, aren't you?"

This is a woman in her late forties. Not unattractive, even with her official DMV Big Hair. She's flirting with me, and I believe it's because I have a bike.

"Why should I paint it black?" I ask her.

"I think *all* old motorcycles should be painted black."

"Where do you get these crazy ideas?"

"Crazy ideas?" She smiles. "Hey, I got all *kinds* of crazy ideas. How many cc's?"

"Twelve hundred."

"Ooh," she says. "Now I *am* impressed."

In a matter of minutes I've completed a transaction I thought might take weeks, and I walk out of the courthouse with the first motorcycle license plate I've had since 1969.

I visit my fenders in East Missoula, find Magoo under the mask with a grinder in his hands. He's dusted with this parrot-green substance and looks like some kind of alien. My fenders are in primer now, with leopardlike spots of epoxy filler. They're sanded and ground down on the high places, and Magoo wants to check the fit of the brake plate to the front fender. Magoo will make a house call tonight just to make sure the fender hangs on the fork correctly. He tells me he plans to "crash" my project, and I'm thrilled. This means I could have my sheet metal back by Monday!

On my way out I see a weird-looking pair of old frames, and Magoo says they are both Hendersons, an obscure four-cylinder motorcycle from out of the 1920s.

"Geez, Magoo. You must be one of the only shops around with *two* Henderson frames sitting there."

"Yeah," he says. "I guess I am. But I'm not sure I like what that says about me."

Chaz compliments me on my progress with the Chief. "And when you get your sheet metal back, Stroker," he says with a grin, "it's going to put you right on your ass."

He tells me again, ruefully, how far in over his head he got to buy Indian Joe.

"How far?"

"*Really* far."

"What, you've got loans with the Gambinos?"

Chaz shakes his head sadly. "No. The people who loaned me the money are really nice. Really, the shadiest part of this whole deal is me."

"Jesus, Chaz. *Now* you tell me." I say this to lighten things up, but Chaz has turned reflective.

"You look around my shop, you see a couple dozen pretty nice old bikes. You know what? Every one of those bikes is the result of overextending, of putting my family's welfare on the line. Twenty years of pain, Fred." He grins ruefully. "That's what you're actually seeing when you check out my pile."

We both let that sink in a moment. He turns back to me. "So when are you going to have that Chief on its feet?"

"I don't know," I tell him. "I'm still waiting for my handlebar risers to come back from California. And I'm really hungover, too."

"You lucky bastard. You went out and got stinking, didn't you?"

"Well, Chaz—it was Bob Dylan's birthday—"

But Chaz is on a tear. "Boy, I wish you could know just what it's like to have to come home to Yvonne after a night like that. Yvonne and two more kids than you've got now."

I want to tell Chaz I *do* have an idea what it's like to come home to someone like Yvonne, who I realize reminds me very much of an old girlfriend, a woman named Lucy. A hard drinker with two small kids—with Lucy, anything was possible, and it gives me the creeps just to think about it.

To change the subject, I tell Chaz I'll give him a hundred bucks for Indian Joe's kicker. I haven't a clue what they're actually worth, but I have yet to see one in a parts catalogue, so I know they're rare.

He tells me a woman named Trisha already promised him sexual favors for Joe's crank.

"Yeah," I say. "But did she promise you *cash*?"

When I get home there is a mysterious-looking packet in the mail. It's from Sara—she's forwarded a folder of old letters my ex-mother-in-law gathered up in the course of a move. There are some junior-high test scores in which it's shown I have a superior vocabulary and capitalization skills. There are a couple of poignant letters from my mother, written to me when I was out wandering, clueless, in the world. But eclipsing everything is a draft of a letter I fired off to my parents over thirty years ago. I had dropped out of Bowdoin that winter, gone to California, where for seven months I worked as a lab assistant on an oceanographic vessel. The first thing I did with my sea pay was buy a Matchless motorcycle from one of the Scripps divers, and I was all set to ride back east on it. But I couldn't register the bike without parental signature, and there was no way in hell Mom and Dad were going to do that. The letter begins:

> *First, an apology for my outburst on the phone. But I felt strongly that you were not treating me as an adult and I reacted in an immature way . . . What you are doing is depriving me of one of the greatest adventures of life, of finding out for oneself, of sitting by the side of the road on a smoking*

motorcycle and kicking myself, or of riding along under a dawn sky, the wind whipping my jacket, watching the blur of trees as I shoot past, the coolness, the newness on my face . . . I won't fly back in four hours of air-conditioned crap now. I shall either cycle back or hitchhike. Whichever, the misery and joy is my own. Please understand that this is not a threat, that I'm simply pushed into proving something which now happens to be more important to me than anything else . . .

CHAPTER 16

A BIKE LIKE A PROM DRESS

In my dream I'm trying to get from Boston to Cape Cod. I'm sitting, waiting for a bus, when Chaz stops to pick me up. He's driving an old Peugeot, and when it's time to start it up, Chaz pushes the car into a ditch, so it's almost on its side. He opens a pet-cock under the carburetor and raw gas pours out. He hands me a revolver, tells me to fire it next to the gas. Cheerfully, he explains that this will ignite the gas and turn the engine over. I take the pistol, fire it a couple times, and several people come out of their houses. I tell them that it's OK, that I'm just trying to start my car. I realize I've managed to shoot a hole in the front tire, and despair of ever making it to Cape Cod.

"Not to worry," says Chaz. Suddenly we're cruising south in a shiny Plymouth Barracuda, a convertible.

"Say, Chaz," I tell him. "This is quite an improvement over the Peugeot."

"Yeah," says Chaz. "The only problem with it is, we're running 1972 plates."

More rain. I've got $2,000 worth of tree work out there and I can't get at it. On a Tuesday Chaz calls, tells me they're about to disconnect his phone service. He tells me that if I want to buy his kicker, I can just make the check out to the phone company.

I know between Indian Joe and the '52 Ford he bought—which he has yet to sell—that Chaz is in a deep hole. So I pilfer $150 from my Magoo paint job fund and drive fast to the Carnal Garage.

My God, what an exciting life this man leads, with its relentless eleventh-hour brinkmanship. And the worst part of it is, it's contagious.

There is much spirited haggling at Chaz's garage; he claims I set a price of $175 the other day. I'm afraid that I did, but since I have no idea what a used Indian crank is actually worth, I deny *remembering* that I did. I allow instead that it might be worth $125. Chaz looks baffled.

"Well, damn," he says. "Nobody's ever tried to work me this way before. Make it a hundred and fifty, you got yourself a kicker."

We horse Indian Joe's frame up on its tail. Chaz begins to count the teeth on the crank, then turns to me and says, "How many teeth on your pinion sprocket?"

I draw a blank. "How many teeth . . . ?" This is something I should have figured out beforehand. But how would *I* know? My pinion sprocket is out in Portland, Oregon. I begin to seize up. I don't want to hand over more cash for what could well be the wrong part.

Meanwhile, Chaz reads my deer-in-the-headlights expression perfectly, and grins. "Are ye *schared,* boy?"

He tosses me a can of WD-40 and a snap ring remover, and I've just begun working to remove Joe's kicker when the cell phone rings and Chaz picks up. There are a long series of uh-uhs, uh-huhs, and then Chaz says crisply, "Well, there's no part that's broken that can't be repaired," and signs off. He looks at me, grins, and says, "By the way, that was Big Cal. It's clear your proximity to Indian Joe disturbed some kind of magnetic field and summoned him up."

"Really? What's Big Cal want?"

"No. What do *I* want," says Chaz. "He was returning my call. That bearded son of a bitch sold me a motor with cracked cases, and he owes me."

With or without Joe's kicker, my Chief seems about as far away from being done as it could get right now. I'm beginning to acknowledge that there are dozens of things standing between me and completion, and that's not counting the unknowns that keep popping up—the questions even the experts can't agree on. Such as whether I need a ten-tooth kicker or a twelve-tooth; such as whether the thirty-two-tooth pinion wheel goes with a magneto Chief or an 80-incher. In the end, finding the right crank is a lot like fitting your sheet metal; anything that even comes close to a fit is cause for celebration.

That night there is a long acid eulogy on KUFM for Timothy Leary, who passed away at seventy-five years of age. They're playing some old Country Joe and the Fish, lots of Grateful Dead, and that Moody Blues song, "Timothy Leary's Dead." It hits me pretty hard for some reason. With Garcia gone and Leary passed away, it's like the '60s have slipped into the realm of pure mythology. I listen to Country Joe's mysterious "Section 43," turn it way up, like I used to. How that crazy music can still fill a garage!

Magoo calls to tell me my sheet metal is finished. I leave the garage doors open all morning to let the lilac fragrance in, while I run around, dunning customers and pumping money into the bank so I can write a plausible check. Then I head for East Missoula.

The paint job is *brilliant*. Jewel-like. Ten feet deep and drop-dead gorgeous. "Uh-oh," I tell Magoo. "I'm not riding this bike anywhere. I might put a scratch in it."

Magoo laughs. He tells me that when he restored his Panhead, everyone told him he was crazy to put so much effort into chrome and paint. "Hey. My first trip, we went down thirty miles of gravel road, and you know, it didn't hurt that bad."

Magoo says I'm rocketing along with my project, that it takes most people two to three years. I feel pretty good about that for a while—again, like I'm winning some kind of race here, but a race with *whom?*

The only thing really holding me back now are my handlebar risers—a ringlike casting that attaches to the steering head where the handlebars are mounted. I sent them off to Starklite weeks ago to have them rebuilt, and if I can only get them back, I can mount the front fender and then the wheels. But I don't have them back. Come to think of it, I don't have my motor, either, and it's all beginning to make me goosey.

I'm ducking Chaz, who is trying to get me to buy into yet another Indian pile—a front end, wheel and brakes, a frame with the seat post cut out, both stands, pedals, and a front fender. I've pretty much lost track of which pile is which, or which pile is financing the others.

"Maybe you can just bankroll the whole thing?" he says without a trace of irony.

We're sitting in Charlie's bar when this conversation occurs. I have just finished pruning my physical therapist's maples, and I'm feeling wrung out. Chaz has little Aydyn in a backpack, and it occurs to me it's the first time I've been in a bar with Chaz. I can tell it makes him nervous.

"Who do I look like, anyway? Daddy Warbucks?"

"Hey," he says. "You're the Big Kahuna here, man."

The barmaid is winsome, blond, with a tattoo of five turtles swimming in a circle on her shoulder. It's about the cutest thing I've ever seen. I take a pull on my Miller. "If I'm the Big Kahuna in your life right now, Chaz, you've got yourself more problems than I thought. And what would I want with another old Indian pile, anyway? I'm still working on the one I have."

Frustrated, Chaz finally gives me the lowdown. "Look, Fred. If I don't get this pile, Bootsy might."

Phoebe's left the family bed and sleeps in a crib for the second night in a row. But today the orthopedist put her in a little hip harness to keep her feet turned out and to keep pressure on her joints. The device involves a couple of stirrups suspended from a chest harness. It's odd-looking, and eight weeks seems like a very long time. People want to know what's wrong with her, and you can't really say "nothing," but we haven't come up with a short answer, either, and it seems awkward. We take her with us to a cocktail party at a playwright's house, up Rattlesnake Creek. We are sitting at a big table with friends, and someone asks, "What color is the bike, Fred?"

"Well," I say. "It's kind of an inky blue-black."

"He means it's midnight blue," says Caroline. "And it looks like taffeta."

"Oh," says a woman friend. "So it's like a prom dress."

The women know exactly what Caroline means. But Jim Crumley turns to me and says sourly, "Wait a minute—are you really gonna let them say your bike looks like a prom dress?"

Everybody's jumping into the rivers. First there was that kid Ryan, early in the winter. Then the guy who jumped off the MacClay bridge, and last night, a man goes swimming in the Blackfoot, up by Red Rock. These rivers are about thirty-eight degrees, huge, swollen, with entire trees floating down them. What would possess a guy to jump into a river that looks like that?

On my birthday I drive out to Huson to rescue a cat named Angus who's been chased up a tall skinny Douglas fir. It all goes pretty smoothly—I spur up, wave a can of food before his nose, zip him in a knapsack, and descend on my rope. This is generally a pretty easy fifty dollars, but when I get home I'm so sore I have to ice both shoulders, and for the first time in my life I'm struck by the idea I may be starting to wear out.

I'm in the kitchen with Caroline, still iced down, when Chaz drops by, and he looks troubled. He says he needs more money. He needs more time. He needs more *sanity* in his life. Nobody says anything, but of course it has to do with Yvonne and him. At some point, I ask Caroline if she'd like me to make her a sandwich.

Chaz's mouth practically falls open. He seems incredulous. "Are you two always this cordial to each other?"

Nearly a year after I went to Portland, Ken calls to tell me my motor is done.

"Christ!" I say. "You're kidding me!"

Ken chuckles. "However," he says, "there were a couple of extras I had to charge you for."

"That's okay, Ken."

"And there was a crack in your primary case and I replaced it with a '39 one."

"That's okay, Ken."

"So what I'll do, I'll swap you that one for yours, just charge you for the MIG weld. Seventy dollars more."

"That's okay, Ken."

"So your total is two thousand, four hundred and ten dollars."

Two thousand, four hundred and ten dollars! It's taken twelve months, but the best price I got of the four rebuild outfits I called was about twice that! I'm very close to weeping. "Ken," I tell him. "That's just fine."

Neil comes over to help me screw sheets of plywood behind the garage windows and install heavy-duty locks. It looks kind of industrial, but I feel much better about leaving for Portland than I did. This is no longer an innocent-looking neighborhood garage. It looks like I'm up to something in there.

We're just finishing when Chaz and Artie come by to look at the bike. Artie walks into the garage and says, "Hey! *Nice* stand!"

He and Chaz admit it's a really good paint job, though they're both careful not to mention the color. Artie points out that I have to take my fork apart again to get my risers on.

"I know that," I tell him.

Artie says, "But once you got that motor in there, you're pretty much home free."

"Well," says Chaz. "There's still lots of other stuff to do."

Artie says, "Yeah, but you get this space right here filled up"—he gestures to space under the tanks and grins—"you don't have many spaces left to fill."

CHAPTER 17

A MOTOR REBORN

THE NIGHT BEFORE WE LEAVE FOR THE COAST, CHAZ DROPS OFF some Scout parts I'm to deliver to Ken. With him is a tiny, cheerful little woman in her seventies.

"Stroker," he says. "This is Minerva, my mom."

She smiles, extends her hand. "I'm pleased to meet you, Mr. Stroker."

"Please," I tell her. "Call me Fred."

"Fred," says Chaz, "Minerva would very much like to see your Chief."

I think of all the seventy-year-old women I know and there are precious few who would actually like to look at a motorcycle, but I open my garage and turn on the lights.

Minerva is politely appreciative of my project, says it's "a lovely motorcycle." Then she tells me about her first ride on the back of Chaz's bike. "I was petrified," she says. "I kept trying to put my arms round his waist, and he kept hollering, 'No, Ma! God! Can't you just hang on to the *seat?*'"

Chaz and I laugh uproariously, then she grows serious. "Really," she says, "it was the worst day of my life when Chaz came home with that first motorcycle."

Again, the miracle of that Pacific air, so fresh and full of promise. Caroline, Phoebe, and I spend the night in Portland with old friends—Rick and Pat and their two children. Rick is an old colleague from Stanford, and he's gone on to have an actual teaching career. I'm frankly envious, but I try not to let it get to me. I watch Caroline and Pat, the way her two kids play with Phoebe, the way this baby seems to open us up to the world. It helps.

A year later, I once again climb the mile-long drive that leads to Ken's hilltop house in Carlton. Ken is unchanged—the same congenial, vigorous man in a sweatshirt and black jeans. His wife Jane comes out, escorts Caroline and Phoebe around the grounds, shows them the rose garden while Ken and I head to his shop.

With so much anxiety, anticipation, and longing expended over a year's time, it's easy to see how this moment could be anticlimactic, but it's hard to exaggerate the effect my rebuilt motor has on me. It's the Lost Chord and the Missing Link rolled into one, and I'm giddy, intoxicated by the sight. What I brought in here was a worn-out fifty-five-year-old piece of machinery. What I'm taking home is immaculate. Pristine. Old CDA1015 is more than just rebuilt. It's Reborn.

I've made a list of questions for Ken, but it's really hard to concentrate. Still, I have enough presence of mind to ask him:

"What about breaking it in?"

"Just don't run it wide open for a while, Fred."

Indian

In the beginning: Fred with parts, Carnal garage, June '95

Chief tanks *before*, June '95

During, July '95

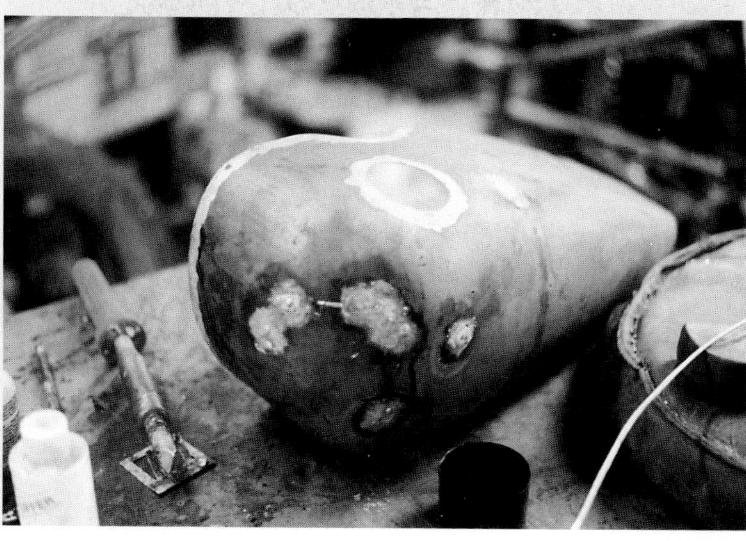

After restoration, August '95

Chief frame and tanks *before*, June '95

Chief frame and tanks *after*, November '95

Magoo fitting new fender, May '96

Indian

Sheet metal mounted, June '96

Fred and Neil mounting engine, July '96

Fred checks head-bracket spacing, July '96

Mounting rear wheel, July '96

Chassis ready for wiring, August '96

The Chief on its feet (with Phoebe Rose), August '96

Indian

The Millennium Flyer

"What's the correct oil?"

"Fifty-weight Castrol, *nondetergent,* in the motor. Ten-weight in the clutch, ninety-weight in the gearbox. Regular unleaded gas."

"How many of these have you done, anyway, Ken?"

"God only knows. I've been rebuilding these motors almost sixty years."

I see a '47 Chief in progress, mention something about the forks being like mine, and Ken says, "No, they're not—yours is a '41."

I say, "No, my *engine* is a '41. The chassis is a '47."

Ken slaps his forehead. "Oh man! I wish I'd known! We maybe could have given you matching numbers!" All those ads for "matching number" Chiefs in the magazines, and here it's so easy to change them, it's almost like a joke. I now believe my Chief is unique for *not* having matching numbers.

Phoebe travels well. She naps most of the time, fusses briefly for a bottle. She can squeal now, and she seems ravenous all the time—last night she ate two bowls of cereal and a half jar of squash, nursed both breasts and one bottle of formula. She's got *cheeks*. She's got a delicious, hiccuppy laugh.

On the way home, the night of the twenty-second, it's the sixteenth anniversary of the night Caroline and I met. We pull into the Sacajawea Inn in Lewiston. I cover the Chief motor with baby paraphernalia and park the car under our window. Then we all have some dinner. There's a VFW convention at the Sacajawea's restaurant, and the tables are full of sweet-faced granddads in their veteran's caps, smoking cigarettes with their buddies.

We put Phoebe to bed, and Caroline and I celebrate with a bottle of good cabernet. When I was a thirty-five-year-old graduate student and she was a twenty-three-year-old adventurer just back from Alaska, we were in the same poetry workshop at the University of Montana. We got together at a full-moon solstice party and we've been together (mostly) ever since—sixteen years now. At first I worried about our age difference, but she was so smart and game, so playful and pretty, I finally couldn't see that it mattered very much.

We consider the new baby, consider the new motor, and wonder what the connection could possibly be. Then we watch an old Fred MacMurray movie, probably postwar, back when he was playing action roles. The movie is about a hard-nosed Rocky Mountain forest ranger who has two gorgeous, spirited women vying for him. He flies around in light planes, pitches lots of woo, chases arsonists, parachutes into fires, cuts down trees, and punches out anyone who seems to have it coming. It speaks well for Caroline that she falls asleep early on this one, yet there is an aspect of this movie that drags me in deeper and deeper—some very familiar, oddly comforting aspect—and finally I understand that it's my old friend, that 1950 boy's dream of what it means to live in the West, and of what it means to be a man. I think of the silliness of these illusions and the years I spent secretly cherishing them, and I'm embarrassed, angered, and somehow touched by it.

On the road home, there are downed trees all along Route 12, from Lolo Hot Springs on. We meet an old fellow at the Lochsa campgrounds who's returning from Missoula, and he tells us he can't wait to get back to Walla Walla.

I ask him why. He says, "Because. It just blows like hell up there in Montana. As far as I'm concerned, you can *have* it."

My message machine is full of tree calls, but I'm too late for most of them. Chaz and a Chevy mechanic they call Speedstick are over this morning, and they seem at least as awed as I am by this bright shiny motor. I've set it on the pickup seat in my garage, and they stroke it, study it, put their fingers in the intake and exhaust ports.

"Those are Chevy valves in there," says Speedstick. "I'm sure of it."

"Wow, Stroker," says Chaz. "You're not gonna want Craig Eddy parking his hunk-of-crap Chief next to yours." He grins. "Hell, you're probably gonna John Wayne him."

With the arrival of the motor, my garage is suddenly full of people: friends, friends of friends, neighbors, friends of neighbors, and, of course, bikers, including Craig Eddy. I don't know if I "John Wayned him" or not, but he gave a little gasp when he saw my Chief and said, "Now, *that* is a thing of beauty."

He and Chaz discuss whether Ken had installed the new oil-tight valve covers, which precipitates more discussion about parts, and then Indians in general, and finally I ask them how many Chiefs are in town these days. Craig and Chaz tally them up in their heads, then finally Chaz says, "How many Chiefs *running*? Yours is likely to be the only one, Fred."

Later that afternoon a half dozen other friends arrive, all wanting to see the bike. I've got an idea for the presentation all worked up. I want to drape the Chief with a black satin sheet that I can whip off, while simultaneously flipping on a pink spotlight and cueing Barry White singing his big hit "We Got It Together, Baby." But I end up settling for an old percale contour sheet, a halogen light, and a Steve Reich tape.

This is all lots of fun, but it begins to make me anxious, because I still have so far to go, and what you see on the stand, with or without the Barry White, is pretty much a mock-up—a lot of shiny parts tacked in place à la Chaz. In reality, when the risers finally arrive, the fork has to come apart and be reassembled, the fenders have to be trimmed, wired, and probably refitted, the electrics and fuel lines have to be dealt with, and the motor has yet to be mounted. I know that it will take me at least a month to get this bike on the road—if I'm very lucky.

It's Chaz's forty-fifth birthday and the whole gang is there—Speedstick and his wife, Eric the roofer, Yvonne's mom, and a couple of young men from the neighborhood, Shane and Kevin. As always, we end up drifting back to the shop, and tonight, under the shoplight on a newly cleared workbench, Chaz has got Indian Joe all apart. Speedstick comes up, talks about all the little ridges, the minute roughness on the castings, about how these lead to cracks, about how the polished rods on Joe are to promote better lubrication and longer wear.

"So," I say, "if a guy has the money, time, and patience, he takes apart his motor, and for the next few years polishes the heck out of everything in there?"

Speedstick considers this, looks at Chaz. "Yeah," he says. "That's about it."

After birthday cake, Aydyn gets cranky. Yvonne picks him up, pulls all his clothes off, lets him run naked for a couple minutes. The little boy is ecstatic; he squeals and laughs insanely.

"No matter what kind of mood he's in," Yvonne says, "all I have to do is pull his clothes off and he feels *great*."

"Well," says Chaz. "I know that always worked for me."

By late June there are young robin parts strewn all around the yard. It's the annual Feast of the Fledglings for the neighborhood cats. Cottonwood fluff is in the air, Russian olive in blossom. Phoebe raises her right leg, flaps her right hand madly while she nurses, babbles to herself. On our last visit, the orthopedist torqued her harness up a whole notch and told us it could easily be a longer therapy than the six additional weeks we now face. The baby is good about it, though you can tell it bothers her. But probably not as much as it bothers us.

CHAPTER 18

RACE TO STURGIS

I GET TIRED OF WAITING FOR CHAZ, AND ON A MONDAY EVENING I enlist the help of my friend, Neil, who doesn't know any more about motorcycles than I do. The two of us horse the fresh two-hundred-pound, 80ci CDA1015 motor into its new frame while the second full moon of the month, a blue moon, rises from behind the mountain. Counting on explicit directions from Ken, I allow myself to believe this motor will slide right in, but it turns out to be a production: We have to shim the frame off the stand for additional clearance, then we have to deal with several fittings that won't quite clear the frame—the transmission drain plug, the oil pump scavenger line, and the throttle cable clip. I would give a lot not to disturb any of Ken's work, but then, before I know it, I'm on my knees with an open-end 7/16-inch, wrenching away. At one point, while Neil supports the motor with his knee, I paw madly through my tools, looking for the 5/8-inch while Neil speaks soothingly: "Now, relax, Fred.

Just take your time, man." and I think, Well bless his heart. My friend is trying to talk me down.

It takes nearly two hours and we leave a couple good scratches in the frame, but finally we set a couple punches in the mounts and secure the engine in place. It's not bolted in yet, but now this project looks like a *motorcycle.*

By moonlight, I lock up the bike and retire to the house. Phoebe makes deep, resonant croaking noises while she swings, while she eats, and this night I have her in stitches, doing my version of the Sailor's Hornpipe in the kitchen. While it's true that I'm probably in some midlife devolutionary spiral, while it's true I miss my students, it's also true that I'm having the time of my life. I know this.

Yesterday Chaz was down the street, pulling out some old arborvitae. It was a job I gave him, and he was working like a man possessed. Or overcaffeinated. He jabbers on about the terrible squeeze he's in for money—it seems they shut off his power and he had to spend his phone bill money to get it turned back on. Now they're about to shut off his phone, and his new Chief pistons are on the way, COD. Talking to Chaz when he's like this is too exhausting. I used to pay my crew once a week, but to accommodate Chaz's crisis-driven lifestyle, I've been paying at the end of the day. Now it seems he wants a check on completion. The constant "Where's the money?" pressure, the incessant calls on that bargain-basement cell phone are beginning to make me feel less like I'm running a tree service, more like I'm dealing crack.

Down at the deli, I see Chaz's red Shovelhead parked with a couple of other Harleys, and then there's Chaz himself, sitting at a sidewalk table with Manny and a couple members of the Butte "Cossacks" Motorcycle Club. I want to go over and tell everyone that I got the engine in the other night, but Chaz is in leather, the Cossacks are in full colors, and in my baggy shorts and Indian T-shirt, I'm suddenly too self-conscious to talk to Chaz and the gang. Do the Cossacks ever wear shorts? I don't know. What if they yank my chain? Laugh at my flip-flops? I get back in my car and flee.

When I get home, I field a call from Yvonne, who's looking all over for Chaz. I lie and tell her I haven't seen him, though these days I don't feel like I owe him much.

I stop by Chaz's with a check, and Phoebe, I, Yvonne, and Aydyn sprawl on the new shag carpet while Chaz rummages in his shop for a set of spare risers. We're through waiting on Starklite. While the babies crawl around us, Yvonne and I take the measure of the year that's gone by and marvel at the two little creatures before us, grabbing each other's toys.

Later on, Chaz and Bummy stop by my place to have a look at the motor, and with barely a word, everyone is suddenly working on the bike. We scour the rust from the risers, prep them, and spray them cadmium silver, and while Bummy pops the front fender off and begins to bolt on the trim strips, Chaz and I can finally assemble the forks correctly—risers in place—and bolt it back on the steering head. Having done that, we forge ahead and mount the handlebars. Then we step back to see what we've done.

"Guess what, Stroker," says Chaz. "Slap the wheels on this dude and you've got yourself a motorcycle."

It's a jolly thought. But I know, and they know, it's going to take a lot more than slapping the wheels on to get this machine on the road.

There are more fledglings in the yard, maybe finches. They fly onto the garage roof, light a moment, stagger back into the air. Friends of Caroline's came in from Alaska and they all went up to the cabin at

Pierce Lake together while I stayed to finish trimming and mounting the fenders. I hope to come up with a twelve-volt generator, too, and I'm feeling a sudden acceleration here. I bolt on the little toolbox and set the chain guard in place; it fits much better but is still slightly off. I eat my lunch in the garage, spend the whole day on my knees, and when I'm through, I'm stiff and I'm beat. I miss Phoebe. I haven't been away from her since she was born.

Meanwhile, across town at the Carnal Garage, a parallel project takes place as Chaz undertakes to rebuild Indian Joe's motor so he can bolt it into his '41 Rainbow Chief. He's decided that with a month left until Sturgis, we should ride down together on our Indians. He seems dedicated, committed. He says he's needed a deadline like this. Can we make it in a month, both of us? Either of us? I haven't a clue.

I eat out that night, and as I'm walking across Higgins to my car, I'm almost bowled over by a brilliant red Chief with Tennessee plates, about the same vintage as my own. It stops at the light right in front of me, and it sounds so great, looks so good that I really feel the need to say something, though I can't think of what. By the forks and trim, I know it has to be a '47 or '48, but I holler out to the guy, "Looking good! What year?"

"'Forty-eight!" he hollers back, and then the light changes and he roars off down the street. I notice that he's converted the authentic Indian configuration to a right-hand throttle and a left-handed shift, and I smirk and think to myself, What a *lightweight*!

Back home I try to watch *Battlefield!* on PBS. It's Montgomery's campaign and the battle of El Alamein. Lots of tanks, sand, guys in shorts. I can't get into it. Could it be that, fifty-two years out, I've finally got my fill of that ghastly war?

I turn off the set. The midsummer evenings go on past ten o'clock. They are voluptuous, scented with linden and Russian olive blossoms.

People are out on their steps, murmuring into the twilight. Our garden is thick with lettuce and the first tomatoes are forming, but all I can think of is what I must do to keep this project going. This afternoon I placed a huge, convulsive parts order with Starklite: exhaust pipes, clutch and throttle linkage, headlight and bracket, seat post and bushings—about 90 percent of the parts I had left to buy, I bought. It will cost me a thousand dollars, and it took Frank half an hour just to write it all down.

Next morning I drive ninety minutes to join Caroline up the Swan River Valley.

Things have changed at Pierce Lake. Someone is firing a large-caliber pistol close by. They're hosing down the woods by the sound of it, and the last clip is rapid-fire. There's a man walking around the lake, blowing a police whistle, and there's a big ugly Rottweiler barking its head off two cabins down. There is active salvage logging, chain saws rapping out over the ridge. Was it that Big Wind that changed everything? In its eleventh hour, has the twentieth century finally arrived here at this tiny mountain lake, blown in by some infernal tornado?

On Monday Chaz and Speedstick stop by, amped up on coffee. I give Chaz his check for the arborvitae, and he and Speedstick study the motor for a moment.

"Let's get this thing in here right," says Chaz, and before I know it, he and Speedstick are swarming over it, doing things faster than I can even think. We get the lower motor mount bolt in, but then it doesn't quite seat on the rear. Speedstick loosens the front bracket and it plops right down, dead center. It's a good snug fit, with only a sixteenth-inch gap between the head bracket, for which I'll need a spacer. Chaz tells me to mount the fenders with flat washers on the inside and washer, lockwasher, and nut on the outside—

and then they're gone, off to wherever people with that much coffee in them go first thing in the morning.

The lawn on the boulevard is burnt brown because we have no trees there, and I sit out late on my front steps with the baby, the dog and cat, and a Coca-Cola. I'm thinking of planting catalpas out there, just because they're different. Or maybe lindens, for their scent, but in the end, probably dwarf fruit trees so Caroline can keep some sun in the front. Friends from down the street were over earlier to see the Chief. I cue the music, do my little sheet-and-light deal.

"My God," says Katherine Kress. "That is a thing of beauty." And since she's a painter and I know painters don't say these things unless they mean them, I finally come to the conclusion that I have done something special with the Chief—that, for the first time in my life, I will have a *Looker*.

I break out the rolling tobacco my friends left behind and roll a smoke. At nine-thirty, half a mile to the east, Mount Sentinel glows huge, bright, and buff-colored in the last of the summer light.

CHAPTER 19

THE CHIEF ON ITS FEET

IT'S UNGODLY HOT. THE LITTLE FAN HUMS AWAY IN THE LIVING room morning and night. More friends show up to view the bike. "My God," says Leonard Robinson, a poet and novelist. "That is a thing of beauty!" I'm starting to wonder what it means that all my friends say exactly the same thing. Does the bike leave them at a loss for words, or did they all get together beforehand and decide on this response?

I'm getting tired of the whole presentation shtick: Cue the music, hit the lights, yank the sheet. I just want to get the Chief done. Or even get it off its stand.

After hours of fittings, I do the final sheet-metal bolt-down, secure the fenders, bumper, support struts, and luggage rack. Next I turn my attention to the front wheel. The wide tire is a tight squeeze in that enclosed fender, and I discover that getting it plumb and getting it to clear the skirts involves another long series of fittings, and every time I horse that big wheel in and out, I'm reminded how, in

1947, the whole idea of lightweight materials didn't enter into the equation at all.

The daytime temperatures hover in the nineties. On a Tuesday, Chaz and Brian and I start a big job up Rattlesnake Creek: the removal of a clump of older cottonwoods, sixty feet tall and close to the house. The trees were hacked in half years before. As a result, a couple are stone dead, a couple more rotten in the top. On my own hazardous tree scale, I give this bunch a perfect 10.

The homeowners run the café that Chaz and I frequent. They are among the nicest customers I've encountered this summer, so I'm dismayed when, with my first cut of the day, I fell a sixty-foot cottonwood uphill, fail to clear the children's custom-made swing set, and take out a two-by-six redwood crossbar. This is plain sloppy tree work, and I *hate* sloppy tree work. Especially when I perform it right in front of the customer and can't even blame it on my crew.

The day continues badly. I'm doing a lot of strenuous climbing, while below me Chaz is screwing around with his chain saws. It bugs me, as there are a couple of other working saws and it is common sense that the ground man does not waste time with repairs when there are other saws running.

By noon I've worked my way up the worst of them, the tree closest to the house. Thirty feet up, a spindly, half-dead top is coming off a big rotten stub. I stick my hand into a cavity the size of a cantaloupe, come out with a fistful of rot, and my heart sinks. It should be taken off in pieces, but I wouldn't trust my weight in this top for God almighty.

With remarkable clarity, I have a vision of ending my tree career right here: I will rope down from this funky widowmaker and never climb another. I will coil my line and pack up my stuff. I will leave these nice people a simple but eloquent note that ends with a line like "Let's all quit while we're still ahead." Then I'll park my truck in front of Charlie's

Bar, where I'll sit and pound down beers while the transients, rummies, and bindlestiffs swarm over my truck and pick over my gear like a flock of crows.

When I come down and study things, I see that on my best day, with the right moon and a stiff wind, there is just enough clearance to snake this ugly tree down the very narrow slot between the carriage light and the corner of the house.

I look around the yard. Most of the stuff I dropped is still there. It's hotter than hell, I'm dehydrated, my clothes are soaked, and Chaz is nowhere in sight. Bummy explains Chaz had to go meet someone.

"Really?" I tell him. "And here I thought we were all doing tree work."

Bummy shrugs, tries to smile. "Well. You know Chaz."

The next day, Chaz is late for work by an hour. I busy myself cutting up the downed wood—something he should have been doing while I was in the trees. By the time he arrives I'm ready to break something.

"Hey. Look here," I tell him. "You're not doing me any favors showing up like this. If you're not into this job, don't bother to show up at all." I say a lot of other things, too, but Chaz hangs in there, weathers the storm without expression. When I finish, he tells me that today he's come to *work,* and with the air somewhat cleared we proceed. Around noon Chaz tells me he was late only because he had to chase the UPS truck down so he could get his COD Chief pistons for Indian Joe.

It's not that I doubt any of this. It's just that this is a day I care nothing at all about motorcycle parts.

Midafternoon, I climb the only tree left—the big rotten spike top I backed off from the day before. I climb it quickly, before I can think about it, tie a rope in it so we can direct the fall. I'm tired, but I'm pumping hard. I want to be done with this job in the worst way, this tree in particular.

My felling saw is heavy as a sack of concrete, and I'm clumsy with it. My notch cut is too deep, the angle is not quite right. Some part of me knows this will be a problem, but another part of me believes I can will this tree down that slot. Suddenly everything slows: The saw is roaring, Chaz is running for the rope. I'm correcting like crazy on the house side, cutting away hinge fast as I can, but the tree goes awry. I wait for Chaz to correct this with the rope, but nothing happens except the old Disaster Slow Motion, and three tons of cottonwood clips the roof with a mighty crash. Shingles fly, the soffit drops, the gutters squeak and twist away. There's a ton of dust in the air, and then silence.

Chaz calls that night to remind me of all the *good* cuts he's seen me make. Maybe he feels guilty because he dropped the rope—I don't know, and I don't even care. True, it could have been worse—I clipped the roof, didn't hit it squarely. But after I've paid for the damage, I will have done the hardest job of the season for free. Worse, after twenty-seven years in the business, I have finally hit a house. Worst of all, it wasn't just any house, but the house of the manager of our favorite caffeine joint in town.

Next morning at coffee, Chaz studies his mug for a moment, scowls, leans across the table, and whispers, "I think someone spit in my latte."

We have a dinner for some artist friends: writer David Duncan and his wife, Adrian Arleo, who's a ceramicist; writer David Cates and his wife, Rosalie, director of the Women's Economic Development Corporation. The summer night is voluptuous, the conversation is wonderful, the company is handsome. We dine in the backyard, drink more wine than we probably should, while a block away, at the park, a brass band oompahs its way through the Wednesday-night concert. The night wind blows, tosses the maples around us. I've got Phoebe on my lap, and I withdraw from the conversation, try to see her in twenty years. I watch tonight's little fin de siècle tableau fade, recede in the distance, and I hope she can remember how lovely it was, her first July on this planet. Back before the turn of the century, way back in the summer of '96.

Chaz says I can make head-bracket spacers out of a beer can, and it's funny—the way I jump at the idea, how I've reached a point where this project feels as if it could use a little shade-tree innovation. So I go back out to the garage, and Phoebe watches curiously while I cut two or three spacers out of a Coors can with a pair of scissors. I slip those under the bracket and bolt the heads down with LocTite. Then I bang out the long engine-mount bolt, mount my new kickstand, and torque it on.

I've lured Magoo over with a can of cadmium spray paint so I can ask him what to do about my chain guard. He studies it a long time without saying anything.

"This is a pain in the ass, right?" I say.

He nods. "Look in the dictionary under 'pain in the ass,' you find a picture of an Indian chain guard." He studies it a while longer, then says, "We can do it slow and careful. On the other hand, we can do it quick and ugly—cut the flange off the front so the chain will clear. Forget that lower mounting bracket altogether. It won't be quite as stable, but then, they never were."

"You know, Magoo. Sometimes quick and ugly's just the thing."

I ask him if the Chiefs are smooth at highway speeds, and he says, "Oh, yeah. Especially with your eighty-inch flywheels. Once you get this thing up and running, you're gonna have a good ride."

He studies the bike a while longer, then says, "I only wish *my* Chief looked this clean."

The squirrels are all going nuts, running berserk in our Douglas fir. Running up and down the fence line, over the rooftops, and down the wires—they're getting on my nerves. It's been sobering, this whole house-bashing episode. It's like somehow maybe I've run my luck. I don't like the way the little girls looked at me the other day when I came to their door with the insurance forms. They were very wary, owlish, like they were thinking, Uh-oh. What's he going to break this time?

Mornings, I take Phoebe out in her stroller. I try to shade her with my body, and while we walk the arbored Missoula streets, I try to keep to the shadows of the maples so she can sleep. Babies like it cool and dark, and it becomes a game we play, this shadow-seeking. I wonder if this is pleasant for Phoebe, and I recall something a friend said, about how one of her first memories was of the sound of her pram wheels on the gravel drive.

Chaz and I work on until we're stopped by problems with the wheel alignment. We get the wheels on their axles OK, but then the tires refuse to turn freely and bind up inside the fenders. Chaz suggests we try to "spread" my freshly painted chrome-trimmed fenders.

"Spread them how?" I say.

Chaz shrugs. "Just reef on them a little bit. Open them up."

"Are you *crazy*?"

Chaz seems stumped, but he suspects there are problems with the alloy wheel, the one I had trued locally. An Indian wheel needs the hub offset half an inch to accommodate the brake drum mount. And, on further examination, we determine that the hub on my Akront wheel isn't offset at all. In fact, it's *inset*. We scratch our heads, leave it till the morning.

The next day I'm in the garage for twelve hours straight. I do nothing all day but work on my bike. My summer evaporates like some little puff of cloud while I sit on a concrete floor, wrenching the weeks away. It occurs to me that I've been without a watch for months now—I plainly have no intention of getting it fixed, I'm off in a zone of my own.

Chaz comes over late one evening with a guy he introduces as "Mellow Monty," his nephew from Great Falls. Monty is lean and wiry in a Resistrol straw hat, clean Wranglers, and pointy-toed boots.

Monty tells the story of how Chaz put him on his Electra Glide when he was only twelve and had him ride it home in the rain because Chaz was too drunk to drive. The problem was, Monty was drunk, too. The cops spotted him running for home, pulled up alongside, and hollered, "Turn your lights on, kid! Turn on your *lights*!"

And Monty had to say, "But I don't know how!"

Chaz has brought over Indian Joe's rear wheel to show how my hub is recessed half an inch from the rim while Joe's sticks out half an inch from the rim. So that's the problem with the rear wheel. But what about the front wheel?

Chaz shakes his head gravely. "We need Magoo over here immediately to straighten this out. This is a panic situation. Sturgis is *two weeks away,* man!"

Once again Magoo makes a house call, and his diagnosis is quick and to the point. On the front wheel, redrill the mounting holes in the fender and clip back the trim-strip mounting screws inside. On the rear wheel, retrue it or replace it.

The park lindens are in flower—are they the last trees to blossom? I can never remember. Some kind of bugs are eating our potatoes, and generally the garden's a mess. I've given up maintaining it, and it's really starting to look that way. Likewise, I've given up on the lawn, given up on car and truck maintenance—given up on everything that doesn't involve the bike or Phoebe.

I spend mornings with Phoebe, afternoons I do enough tree work to pay the bills, and the rest of my time is spent in the shop. One afternoon I'm at my friend Connie's to look at her willow, and she says, "I'm glad to see you get out of that garage, where you're holed up all the time, making love to your bike."

"What? Making love to it?"

"Oh, cut it out," she says, exasperated. "Everybody knows that's what you do."

At every shop in town it's the same story: Nobody can get to my wheel for the next three weeks. Finally I call Starklite and talk to Frank. He can't fix my wheel in twelve days either. He does, however, have a complete rebuild sitting right in front of him, up for grabs.

"I'll take it," I tell him. "How much?"

"Five hundred bucks," says Frank.

My heart nearly stops. If I weren't trying to make Sturgis, I would call Frank a dirty name. But I'm over a barrel, so I cowboy up and put it on my Gold Card, along with the thousands of dollars in other parts I mean to pay off someday.

Chaz rides over on his Shovelhead, wearing a T-shirt that says "Thundering Dummies Motorcycle Club." Out in the garage he fondles my latest parts shipment—the exhaust pipes, ignition switch, and seat post.

"My God," says Chaz. "I've never *seen* so much nice new stuff." And then we get to work.

The original seat-post bushing is fused inside the frame, and we have to peel it out in sheets with a pair of pliers and a penknife. While we work, Chaz unloads. More about Yvonne: her migraines, the new medication she's strung out on. The ongoing crisis with child care. The ongoing crisis with money. Christ, I think. This is getting too close for comfort. With my Gold Card maxed out and my summer in ruins, I'm beginning to wonder what we're doing out here, two middle-aged guys in their spectacles, working on a fifty-year-old bike while their lives crash and burn.

Eleven days to Sturgis. I've got too many new parts, and I'm concerned about the feeling of throwing this bike together. I need to drag my foot, slow things down. I'm trying hard to finish, but I'm not prepared to go insane, to turn a good-looking project into some kind of rolling disaster.

Caroline came out to the garage last night while I was working. She has the baby on her hip and she's waving my Gold Card bill all around. It seems my account is over the limit, and she says something like "What are we going to do about all this business, Fred?"

"Hold it right there, honey," I tell her. "I want to remember you like this always."

We're closing on August. The fan's on high. Caragana pods are crackling and popping in the heat. This morning's news says they are "optimistic" about finding the flight recorder for TWA 800. First it was ValuJet. Now TWA. There are still six weeks to go, but so far this is the summer of the Black Box.

Early in the morning, Chaz comes over with a strapping young fellow named Shane. Shane and his brother, Kevin, are neighbors of Chaz's. Shane is an Army machinist stationed at Fort Bliss. I put Phoebe in her stroller and we head for the garage to look at the bike. Chaz tells me the wiring probably comes next, and of all the things I feel inept about, electrical matters are at the top of the list. I watch Chaz and Shane clip the wiring harness to the frame and we stand there uselessly with a schematic from a parts catalogue, trying to make sense of it.

That night I'm looking for something to do by myself, something besides wiring. I decide to put the kicker stop on, which has been rattling around my garage from the start. I find a two-inch 5/16 s and it's really tight. Are the threads full of paint? I grind the bolt briefly on either side so the threads will cut, a Parts Father trick I learned through Chaz. It's a quarter inch too long, but instead of waiting for morning when the hardware stores open, I lop it off with a hacksaw, file away the burr, and to my astonishment, I have a perfect fit. I do the same thing with the headlight bracket bolt, and in a half hour I've overcome obstacles that would have stopped me cold the week before. It's late at night and I'm out here by myself, innovating. Nobody ever told me I could innovate. It's just me, my wits, and this bike, all coming together on a summer's night. I understand I've crossed a kind of threshold with this project—that, while I still long to turn everything over to some really competent guy who can handle the tricky parts, more and more that really competent guy ends up being *me*.

My new wheel arrives, UPS overnight, and Phoebe and I take it to a cycle place called Shopworks to get the tire mounted on. The counterman and I swap baby stories. He tells me his sixteen-month-old stands at the window, points to his dad's Harley, and goes "Vroom! Vroom!" till his mom can hardly stand it.

I'm back in my shop, mounting the generator, when I hear a couple of bikes pull up—Chaz and a kid they call Sneezy, on their Shovelheads, and what a beautiful pair they make! Chaz's is deep blood-red, Sneezy's is brilliant aqua with pale blue flames.

"Your bike," I tell him. "It's gorgeous."

"Thanks," says Sneezy. "It was my father's."

Sneezy's ready to ride down with us. He seems ready to leave today. He's in his twenties, a petroleum engineer—on four weeks and off for two. I suddenly feel a terrific rush of excitement for this whole event. The bikes are gorgeous, the company's good. For the first time I'm feeling excited about this ride, and for the first time in a while, I feel I've lucked out, having Chaz as my guide.

Back at Shopworks, the counterman says they mounted my wheel for just twelve bucks and they slipped me the chrome balancing weights for free.

"That's because it's an *Indian,*" he says fiercely. "Now, if you were some yuppie coming in here with your Jap bike wheel, it'd be twice that much."

Eight days to go and counting. The Chief is taking shape. I mount the giant chrome headlamp and Caroline says, "Now it's got eyes!" I put in another parts order for a dimmer switch and a generator drive belt. Nobody's really tackled the electrics yet, but meanwhile parts keep arriving: loom tube, center stand, air cleaner, and wiring clips.

Chaz and I need a big wrench to replace a worn drive sprocket, and we go back to his shop in search of tools and hardware. Yvonne's been sick, and it's a domestic vortex. It can be risky going over there. We may never find a way back out, but we decide to risk it.

Yvonne is napping with Aydyn on the shag carpet. She wakes up angry because the van ran out of gas on her.

"I was *really* mad at you an hour ago," she says crossly. "Why don't you ever put more than three bucks' worth of gas in that van?"

It's more than I can stand, and I retreat back to his shop.

Chaz follows in a moment, shakes his head, and says, "*She* runs out of gas, and she's mad at *me*."

I study his 1941 Chief for the loom and generator mounts. I feel guilty about Yvonne. We always have to give her the slip somehow. Does she hate me? I don't know. She might—incredible, the whirlwind nature of this project. I know the way it exhausts everything—your time, your money. Even your marriage.

We grab the big wrench and a drawer full of bolts and we're off again to gas the van. I follow him in my Subaru, realize with a start I'm running on empty myself.

Back home there's a note telling me Caroline and her friend Beth have taken Phoebe off for a swim in the Bitterroot River. I worry about them briefly, since it's such an unlucky season for river swimmers so far, but I suppose it's better than worrying about bombs. When I think of this summer long from now, it will be as the exploding summer: Unabombers, pipe bombs, truck bombs, mail bombs, airplane bombs. The astounding exploding summer—the Big Bang summer that my Chief went together.

There are thundershowers in the afternoon. It slakes this burnt-up little town, and afterward it smells so good. Phoebe's restless, napping very lightly. Yesterday she wouldn't go down at all. Sneezy shows up out of nowhere. He's bored, restless, and wonders if I need any help. I put Phoebe in her stroller, take her to the garage with a bottle of formula while Sneezy and I thread the horn and dimmer-switch electrics through the handlebars. We study the schematic and figure out most of the dashboard wiring, while Sneezy tells me as much as he dares about the great Chaz and Bootsy feud: how Chaz turned Bootsy on to an especially nice Chief and Bootsy bought it, then turned around and sold it again for a profit.

"What's wrong with that?" I say.

Sneezy gives me a funny look. "Chaz turned him on to that bike as a friend, because he thought Bootsy'd keep it, not turn around and sell it. To Chaz, that's betrayal."

Aydyn's first birthday. Chaz's place is full of neighbors and relatives. There's cake for everyone else, and Aydyn has his own Winnie the Pooh cake, which he literally dives into, then starts to cry. It's not clear what he was expecting.

I drift back to the shop, where Chaz and Bummy are having a discussion about whether or not there's a gasket compound known as Gorilla Snot.

"There's no such product," Chaz declares.

"I'll bet if you walk into any parts store in California and ask for Gorilla Snot, they'll hand you a tube of that bright yellow 3M gasket compound," counters Bummy.

"Okay, but they don't *market* it under that name."

Chaz is looking for a steel strap for my voltage regulator when Yvonne emerges from the hallway. She is dark-eyed, lovely. She looks good-naturedly piqued, too.

"What are you guys all doing out here?" she says, mostly to Chaz. "The party's out *there*."

On the way back to the party, Chaz says, "You know what, Fred? It seems to me you're running out of reasons not to put that Chief on its feet."

The next morning Chaz appears with the strapping neighbor kids, Kevin and Shane. The four of us fumble around beneath the homemade stand, removing all the clamps, then we each grab a corner and hoist the Chief off the stand.

Funny. A fully equipped Chief weighs close to six hundred pounds, but I have no sense of lifting anything that heavy. Before I know it, we've eased it onto the garage floor, and for the first time, the motorcycle now rests on its tires, leans on its kickstand. How *low* this bike sits, and how *blue* it is! Long after everyone else has left, I walk around and around it, trying to figure out what just happened. It's like we turned some kind of mechanical objet d'art into a vehicle. At this point, the bike is no longer the Chief. It is now the Millennium Flyer.

We invite several people over for Phoebe's naming ceremony; Caroline's parents, her brother, our neighbors, a Methodist minister, and Phoebe's namesake, Caroline's great-aunt Phoebe. We stumble through nearly every aspect of it, Caroline and I. People are late. It rains, so we have to move the party indoors. Caroline burns the pesto, I underestimate the fire for the steaks. The Reverend gets so hungry, he comes out to watch me cook them. People are starving to death. As part of the ceremony, we want to read a stanza of Galway Kinnell's "Under the Maud Moon." I wanted to read the sixth stanza, but I can't, because I know it will make me weep. Caroline ends up reading the last one, the grim one, by accident:

And in the days
when you find yourself orphaned,
emptied
of all wind-singing, of light,
the pieces of cursed bread on your tongue,

may there come back to you
a voice,
spectral, calling you
sister!...

CHAPTER 20

WAY PRIMORDIAL

ALL DAY LONG YOU CAN HEAR THE BIG HARLEYS BOOM THROUGH town on their way to Sturgis, and there's a story on the radio about an eastbound cyclist killed just this morning.

We're finishing dinner, the three of us, when I hear the distinctive sound of an Indian motor—a roaring clattering sound, like a soup spoon stuck in a dishwasher, and when I look out the window, there's Chaz in leathers, riding his 1940 Chief across my lawn. This is surprising, because last I'd heard it had been declared unridable.

"Wow," I say. "What did you do? Transplant Indian Joe's motor?"

"Yeah," says Chaz. "It was tricky, too. I had to do it while they were both still running."

"Seriously?"

Chaz scowls. "Joe's boogered. I put the wrong bearings in and I have to go back to square one."

"How'd you get this thing running?"

"Well, I thought it had cracked cases," he grins, "but then I decided it couldn't afford to have cracked cases."

"You think it'll make it all the way to South Dakota?"

"It certainly has before," he says crisply.

It's *impressive*—Chaz in his leathers, Chaz with his Chief. I feel a deep, jarring longing to be on the road.

Out in the garage, we do a kind of parts triage, try to pick all the things we can leave off to help get my Chief on the road a bit faster:

Can I make it down without a muffler?

Absolutely.

Can I make it down without the chain guard?

Absolutely.

But the brake-light control mounts on the chain guard. Can I make it down without a brake light?

Absolutely.

This having been decided, we go to work on the brake linkage. We run out of parts a couple of times, but we end up cannibalizing fittings off the chassis of Indian Joe, who has taken up temporary residence in my garage. When the brakes are done, we go on to the electrics. It's a funny thing—this technology's been around a hundred years, but, really, the way so many people throw up their hands, it might as well be some kind of juju.

It's ten P.M., but Chaz calls up Kevin and Shane, and within minutes they arrive with Shane's circuit tester. We run all the wires, figure out what goes where, and in the process determine that my dimmer switch is haywire, so I can only run high beams.

Can I make it to Sturgis with only high beams?

Chaz nods. "Low beams are for pussies."

I dash out to buy us a six-pack of Coke, and by the time I return, the ignition switch is wired in and so is the amp meter.

Chaz turns on the switch and the taillight winks on, burning a brilliant violet against the midnight-blue fender. What a miraculous, startling moment it is.

We work till nearly midnight, and later on I lie in bed, worrying. I'm worried because we're getting really close. If UPS brings my oil lines in the next couple of days, we can actually start the Chief up, and I wonder if anyone's ready for that, especially me.

The following night I'm alone in my garage, tightening up the lug bolts, inspecting the linkage, and generally diddling around till I'm bored and put down my wrenches. I pop in an ancient Ike and Tina Turner tape and decide to have a drink. I've been at this restoration for better than a year now—since the bike was just a pile of junk under a bare bulb, so ugly even the cat wouldn't whizz on it, and he'll whizz on anything. I've scraped it, sanded it, drilled it, and filled it. I've straightened it, bent it, primed it and timed it. In the process, I've been ripped off by unscrupulous parts guys, humiliated by my own ignorance, dunned by Gold Card for the $10,000 worth of parts charges I've racked up.

I have another drink. Tina's singing about how there's this guy, that she'll "work my fingers right down to the bone, do anything to please him right or wrong."

I suck at my glass of gin and think, *Tell* it, girl.

Over thirteen months I've seen the Chief completely apart and partly complete, and everything in between. But with all the fittings and refittings, bolting ons and bolting offs, I've yet to see the Chief together. Tonight's the night.

I bolt on the freshly upholstered seat I just got in the mail, the one with the black leather fringe and the single, understated row of studs. I pour another drink, even though it's a Monday night. I know I'll just have to take it all apart again, but I'm onto something here. I bolt the gas tanks to the frame, screw the insignia badges in place. I bolt on the headlight, the shift lever and footboards, then I turn off all the lights but the overhead flood. I want to see what I've got here. I *need* to see what I've got.

What I've got is startling. The Chief sits impossibly low. It's long and dark and sleek—a smoky, skinklike blue-black that's miles deep. It's powerful-looking, dangerous, and tantalizing. But mainly, the Chief is beautiful beyond my wildest dreams. Maybe too beautiful to ride, I don't know. It bothers me that I don't really know what this machine does yet.

I turn off the music. All this cheetah-in-heat stuff is hard on the nerves. I walk to the front of the garage to get some air. Once more I hear the big bikes passing through the night. I'm suddenly very tired. It's August 6. The summer is nearly past. There's too much left to do, and we're not going to make Sturgis this year.

I look back at the Chief. So, Motorcycle. What exactly *do* you do, you great big gorgeous hunk of machine? Are you a fiasco or are you the real McCoy?

And with that I lock up, hit the lights, return to the house. It's great to be out of the garage. I'm *sick* of the damn garage. Badly as I want to go to Sturgis, I realize, sitting there in the tub, that there's a substantial part of me that would just as soon stay home and play with little Phoebe.

Chaz points out that I've been walking around for the past several days, heaving these long, sibilant sighs, just like a little old man. I wasn't aware of it. I'd never tell Chaz, but I understand immediately that what I'm doing is a version of the breathing exercise Caroline and I practiced in Lamaze class, the one they call the Heehee-hoo: Heehee, breath in. Hooo, breath out.

I'm worried about money and the many jobs I've pushed aside to finish this stupid machine. Of course, I'm worried about the machine, too, and everything in between—including all my friends. For example, Chaz is hiding out in my garage. Yvonne is looking for him and so is a client he's run afoul of. He brings fresh parts, news of Bummy, whose wife just kicked him out of the house, and Shane, who rolled his Bronco on the interstate and had to be medevaced out for plastic surgery.

"Christ!" I tell him. "This time of year! This terrible dog-day vortex! What's next?"

Chaz considers this. "Well," he says. "That nice Linkert carburetor I showed you? The one I got out of Joe? It's cracked. But I found this one instead."

I look at this new carb. It's corroded and tarnished. The fittings are loose; it's covered with cobwebs, dust, and bug feces. When Chaz blows on it, an indignant-looking beetle crawls out. Chaz prepares to bolt it on.

"Whoa," I say. "Aren't we even going to clean this out?"

Chaz gives me a look that suggests he is just beginning to appreciate how truly anal a person can be. "Well, suit yourself, Stroker," he says. "But the air cleaner covers it. Nobody's going to even see it."

There are problems with the oil lines. We've pilfered tank fittings off Indian Joe, but the old fittings are incompatible with my brand-new lines, so while I install the ignition wire conduit, he's tossing things away, rebending the lines in a dizzyingly slapdash and careless manner.

Nothing quite seems to fit, and Chaz is moving so fast, it makes my head hurt. Now the gas feed won't line up because the intake manifold hasn't yet been tightened. Chaz is cheery in the face of all this chaos, but why shouldn't he be, I think. It's not *his* fifteen thousand. Jesus, I think. How'd I end up with this clown?

He reads my mind, croaks at me in his best Royal Dano voice, "Are ye *schared,* boy?"

I don't answer him. All I can think is, Breath in, breath out. Hee-hee-hoo.

His cell phone lies there on the bench, beeping and spitting, while we work on until we finally hit the wall: It's the intake manifold. This is a critical piece, and it won't quite line up between the two cylinders. For the first time ever, Chaz seems thrown. He's afraid to force the crush nuts, because if those threads are damaged, the restoration is ruined.

We're covered with sweat. There's oil-soaked cat litter clinging to my arms from lying on the floor, and my guts begin to churn.

"Know what we're going to have to do?" says Chaz.

"What?" I say. "Get some counseling?"

"We're going to have to loosen these cylinders at the base and crank them around so the manifold will fit."

"You're telling me we'll have to undo everything we've done in the past week."

"Yeah," says Chaz. "Looks like we will."

"And we'll have to undo Ken's work, too."

"Yes," says Chaz. "That's a fact."

"I'm sorry," I tell him. "That's just not an option."

There's a terrible moment of silence. "Well," says Chaz, reasonably. "Let's call Magoo, then, see what he thinks."

Chaz rides off to placate Yvonne and Magoo rides up on his '53 Panhead. He wears a leather cyclist's cap, and with his goatee and wire-rimmed glasses, he has a distinctly Bolshevik look. He shuts down his Panhead, rummages briefly through his pannier bags for a small wire brush and a bastard file. I'm always reassured with Magoo on the scene. He's quiet, focused, confident, and serene.

Beneath the halogen light, he studies the manifold threads carefully, files at a burr, studies the threads again.

I tell him that when the crush nuts wouldn't line up, Chaz freaked out.

"Yeah," says Magoo. "Well, he *should* have. That's one place you can really screw up a motor."

He says the manifold threads are clogged a bit from the plating, a little tight, but OK. He grins "The thing about Chaz is, he's just not *used* to new parts. Everything he uses is mostly worn out."

We have a beer. I watch Magoo coax the crush nuts on and off the manifold with WD-40, watch the way he works the nut back and forth so patiently.

Chaz is back in time for Magoo's diagnosis, which is the same as his own: The cylinders must be off center.

Somehow, with the delivery of this second opinion, it is now a fact. For me, it's the equivalent of open-heart surgery, but there are no options left except to undo everything we've done in the past week and undo Ken's work, too. Heehee-hoo.

With the three of us wrenching, it goes fast. In an hour's time, we're slacking the anchor bolts on the front cylinder. Chaz grabs the jug, turns it lightly, deftly. Magoo tries the manifold again. There's a breathless moment, then: "Perfect!"

In another hour, the bike is back together, then Magoo takes a beer break. I take one too. We're covered with sweat, all of us. We've been in there for hours. Nobody says it, but the bike is almost ready. Chaz puts his Coke down and says, "Okay. Now, where's the oil?"

"I haven't got any," I tell him.

"Go grab two quarts of Valvoline Racing," says Chaz.

"Ken says use nondetergent."

"Fuck Ken."

"But —"

"Let him use nondetergent. You can't *get* nondetergent."

"Well, aircraft oil is nondetergent —"

"Jesus. FUCK aircraft oil!" Chaz says sharply.

I'm thinking all kinds of things, mostly what Ken said about the dire consequence of anything but nondetergent, but none of it seems relevant anymore. We're right in the here and now, in the slot. Ken isn't here, and Chaz is somehow running the show.

I return with the oil, and Chaz is rigging a jumper wire from a Harley battery to my coil. My garage seems like a dreamscape. I kind of want this to happen right now, but mostly I really don't. I'm thirteen long months into this, yet it's all going too fast.

"Okay, we've got electrics," says Chaz.

"Get a fire extinguisher ready," says Magoo, and the next thing I know, I'm straddling the Flyer.

Chaz fiddles with the carb, says "*Crank* it," and I jump on the big Indian kicker with all my weight.

Nothing.

"Give it throttle."

I twist the throttle about halfway, jump on the crank again.

Nothing.

I reach down, switch the positions of the plug wires, and crank a third time. In a heartbeat, three hundred nights in this tiny garage are distilled into a thunderclap of ignition, a staggered series of explosions that build quickly to a magnificent, window-shattering, wall-sundering bellow.

On my left, Chaz motions for me to throttle down. On my right, Magoo peers into the oil tank to see if the pump is working. I twist the throttle back and the bellowing ebbs slightly. I seem to be having an out-of-body experience. Magoo listens thoughtfully, as if to a passage of chamber music. Chaz grins like a hyena.

I kill the motor; everything stops.

"What'd you think of *that*?" says Chaz.

The next day, a friend will ask me the same question. "Wow," I'll tell him. "It was *way* primordial." But that night, I don't say anything at all. All I really remember about it was that when the smoke finally cleared, Caroline and Yvonne had appeared and they were holding the babies, round-eyed and silent, at the mouth of the garage.

A day later I bump into my neighbor, Bill, an old truck driver who lives across the street. He asks me how the bike's coming, and I tell him pretty good.

Bill says, "Yeah, I heard you guys start it up the other night. I knew immediately it had to be you." Then he grins. "Man," he says, reverently. "It sounded like a Freightliner cranking up over there."

At coffee the next morning there's Chaz's battered Rainbow Chief parked between Steve LaRance's futuristic Buell and a funky old Suzuki with household belongings tarped to the luggage rack. Chaz is talking to LaRance, who looks spiffy in his Dockers and Harley-Davidson jacket and what looks like a Harley-Davidson attaché case. When I sit down with them, Chaz digs around in his pocket and hands me an Indian front axle nut that was all nicely polished.

LaRance guffaws. "See that? He's giving you his left nut." Then he turns to Chaz. "There's something I've always wondered about."

"What?" says Chaz.

"You've got, like, what . . . half a dozen running bikes to pick from? It must be hard to choose which bike every morning."

"Naah," says Chaz. "That's *easy*. I just pick the one I think is most likely to make it to the coffee shop."

LaRance gets up, slips on his helmet. We watch him strap the attaché case to his Buell, start it up, and accelerate briskly into the morning traffic. When he's gone, Chaz's face grows serious. He tells me that Bummy had a heart attack the day before.

"You're kidding!"

"Uh-uh. I should have seen it coming yesterday. He had all the classic symptoms: vomiting, shortness of breath."

"The guy's barely forty years old," I say.

"I guess that doesn't matter very much, does it?" Chaz sips his espresso. He says the other thing he wants to tell me is, he's not going to make it to Sturgis this year. He shakes his head. "There's not enough money and there's not enough time, Fred. I hope you're not too disappointed."

"No," I tell him. "To tell you the truth, I'm *relieved*."

That night I get a phone call from Sneezy. It's hard to hear him for all the ZZ Top music and biker cackling, but he's calling from the Broken Spoke Bar in Sturgis. "Hey," he says. "Where the hell *are* you guys?"

I feel bad. The kid was actually expecting us. He's reserved a campsite for us and everything. I explain our situation the best I can, and Sneezy becomes politely philosophical. "Oh, well," he says. "Next year when I've got my Knucklehead done, we'll all try it again."

While I'm still on the phone, Chaz swings by on his Shovelhead and drops some stuff off in front of my garage. Then, like some parts fairy, he's gone before I can get out the door to say hello.

The nights are cool enough for the eiderdown. The county fair is in full swing and it's the height of the Perseid meteor shower. The daytime temperatures are into the nineties, and I can't shake the feeling that this heat is a kind of membrane between us and the rest of the year.

"Blackouts in Six States as Temperatures Soar," the headlines read. Bummy is back on the job. At one point he's reading us his medication instructions, which begin: "So you've had a heart attack." The air is smoke-clogged from wildfires around Corvallis and Canyon Ferry. The morning light is eerie, eclipse-like.

There's the smell of grass gone to seed, and despite the hot afternoons, cold mornings with wood smoke in the air have arrived. The summer has fled. I see the beat-up state of our garden and I identify with it. It seems we've just completed an enormous breakneck cycle, and I feel exhausted.

Chaz and I stop off for a double shot of espresso, and Magoo's friend Karen shows up. She tells us that the other night she asked Magoo if we were gonna make it to Sturgis. Magoo told her the bike wouldn't be done in time. "Fred's not like Chaz," he told her. "He's gonna do it *right,* he's not just going to slap everything together."

Chaz bursts out laughing. When he finally catches his breath, he pantomimes jamming a couple of wires together and Karen and I burst into laughter, too. Then he says, "You know, the worst part about a reputation like mine is, it's only about half deserved."

"Have you ridden your Indian yet?" Karen asks me.

I tell her I haven't, and she looks perplexed. "Jeez," she says. "Maybe I'll come over there and ride it for you."

As we leave there, I wonder how it's possible that everyone in town knows I'm stalling on this.

CHAPTER 21

RIDING THE MILLENNIUM FLYER

AT THE GAS PUMP I SWING A LEG OVER THE FLYER AND PREPARE to start it up. There is a muffled rattle from my jacket pockets, where I've squirreled away enough extra bolts, cotter pins, and hand tools to put the whole bike back together again—if it comes to that. It's the big Indian's maiden voyage, and about the only thing I didn't manage to cram into my pockets was the large rubber mallet that, for a mechanic of my particular abilities, had become such an essential part of the restoration.

I reach down beneath the gas tanks, turn on the petcocks, close the choke, crack the throttle, and try to remember the various other steps of the starting drill. On an Indian motor there are anywhere from four to ten steps, depending on whether the motor is warm, cold, or somewhere in between, and so far, in the day or two I've been riding it, I've never failed to forget at least one.

The pair of Harleys I'm with have electric starters , and they light up instantly, eagerly, so that I'm engulfed by their merry rumblings as I crank away on the Indian's industrial-size kicker with little effect. Finally, somewhere between the half-throttle and the quarter-choke, I lose track of what I'm doing. The big motor kicks back churlishly, nearly flinging me off the bike. In a matter of a minute or two, I've worked up a pretty good sweat and the other motorists at the pump are beginning to regard me with curiosity. Chaz does a quick assessment of the situation, shuts down his Harley, trots over, waves me off my bike.

"Why?" I say.

He says, "Because. You'd better save yourself for later."

I can't say this doesn't ring ominously for me, but nevertheless, I'm glad for the help.

Chaz quickly straddles my Chief and stomps the kicker with a kind of outlaw brio. On the second attempt the bike fires up, settles into a contented syncopated idle. He hands it back over to me.

"What exactly did you just do?" I ask him.

"The spark. You forgot to retard the spark."

Of course. The *spark*. Well, I think with some relief, at least it's not my kicking technique. My own special invention, my kicking technique involves a kind of mincing sidesaddle hop-step. I suspect that it looks ridiculous but that my friends are too polite to point this out.

Bummy and Chaz (with Yvonne on the back) wheel their Harleys smartly around, blip their throttles, ride to the edge of the filling station's asphalt apron, and wait. Soon I realize they are waiting for me. They want me to lead so that if I break down they will be there to help. I wheel the Flyer around and blip the motor gamely. Then I cowboy up and prepare to launch my pristine six-hundred-pound midnight-blue and chrome Indian Chief into the heart of Labor Day traffic.

And here is where the Indian's uniquely configured controls have the power to transform a quotidian enterprise like launching the bike into an adventure. Tricky enough to earn the epithet "suicide shifter," the concept of a hand-shift, foot-clutch motorcycle is challenging all by itself. But in a Draconian attempt to inspire brand loyalty, the Indian factory installed their throttles on the left, their shifters on the right—the mirror opposite of any motorcycle ever produced. Designed to cull out all but the most dexterous Harley riders and certain extraterrestrials, these controls produce the kind of synaptic meltdown I haven't experienced since 1971, which was the summer I spent trying to teach myself to juggle. In the couple of days I've been at it, each stop sign I encountered produced some new type of aberrant riding: killing the bike when I wanted to speed up; gassing it when I meant to slow down; gritting my teeth, revving the big motor till it bellowed, then slipping the clutch till it smoked and stank. In addition to the exotic throttle placement, there is another, more insidious distinction to the Indian controls, which is the reversal of the logical operation of clutching. "Toe to go," a Harley rider not familiar with the Indian told me. "What's the problem?" By this he means that with the similar rocker-type clutch bar on a vintage Harley, you punch the heel plate to disengage, the toe to reengage. But with the Indian, it's the *heel* that reengages the clutch. And the pressure point (I won't discover it for the next couple of weeks) is somewhere in the last quarter inch of play.

I could have converted the controls—lots of restorers do. But in an effort to enter into the spirit of the thing, I opted for the authentic factory style. And so I only have myself to blame as I sit here in my new leathers on this gorgeous Labor Day morning, a mere hundred feet from Ole's beer depot, a real accident waiting to happen. I'm blipping the throttle, smoking the clutch. I rev it and slip it, slip it and rev it until I can hardly stand it, but somehow, I'm still not moving! I paddle feebly at the tarmac with my right foot in an effort to push off, fairly willing the big cycle to move as I watch my traffic window close up. I see a Ryder van bearing down, and in the blink of an eye I see that it's loaded with grinning Californians, all in cowboy hats, and I'm thinking, Christ, no *wonder* this motorcycle is extinct. It killed off all its riders!

I concentrate, *ease* down on the clutch plate, and then suddenly, magically, there's the wind in my face and I'm tooling down Southwest Higgins, in the lead. Before I know it, I've even shifted into second gear! Chaz has suggested that we make another stop at a shopping mall a couple miles ahead, just to double check the bike. But I'd do just about anything to not go through another traffic launch again—and besides, I've established a kind of rhythm. I'm hitting the lights as they go to green and rolling on through. By the time we reach the mall I give Chaz the thumbs-up and we keep going. I'm beginning to sense daylight up ahead, and I keep thinking, Man! If we can just make it to the open road!

But now here we are, at a dead stop at the end of Thirty-ninth. We're only fifty feet to 93 Southbound, but the flow of holiday traffic is running like a spring tide. There's no stoplight to help us and it's coming from both directions, about forty-five miles per hour. My heart sinks like an anvil. Within sight is the open road, with only one more launch to get through. But without a hint of a break, after five minutes of waiting, Chaz gets off his Harley, stands behind me, and prepares to *push* me out with a rolling launch, much as you would launch a kid on his training wheels. I don't even care that it's undignified. I just want to keep moving.

Another five minutes pass, and Yvonne heaves a sigh I can hear above the rumble of the bikes. She slides off the back of Chaz's Electra Glide, strolls into the traffic with the insouciance of someone checking out a yard sale. Finally she comes to a stop in the middle of the northbound lanes, where she faces down the motorists with a look that seems to say, "Hey. What the fuck is *wrong* with you people? We're trying to get *out* of here."

I watch, fascinated, as Yvonne raises her hands. Gradually, incredibly, the traffic slows down, very nearly stops. It's a marvelous performance, quite a bit like Moses—if Moses had an attitude and wore black leather.

Maybe Chaz pushes me, maybe he doesn't. I slip the clutch, gun the motor, *will* the bike across two lanes of traffic, and launch myself southbound, into the Highway Experience.

If you haven't ridden, it's hard to explain the similarity between motorcycles and flight. Maybe it's the leathers, maybe it's the exposure, maybe it's the closeness to the machine. Maybe it's just the wind. But immediately we are headed south in a loose formation, and after the Thirty-ninth Street lights and traffic I feel festive, *unleashed.* As we bowl along toward the outskirts of town, I'm watching the car dealers, taco joints, Mini Marts, and maximalls slip away into my mirrors and the buff-colored bench, the lush river bottoms of the Bitterroot open up to us. We motor blithely through the last light at Wal-Mart and I attempt my first shift into third gear, which after such a clean launch seems almost too much to hope for. I try it a couple of times and miss, then suddenly the shifter seems to pop into gear on its own, as if the Flyer had finally just gone ahead and shifted without me. The second-gear vibration ceases and the exhaust note falls behind me now. Except for the distant chatter of the valve train, there is mostly the sound of the wind as the big motor lopes along easily, and I begin to relax.

Chaz and Yvonne ride up alongside me. Since I don't have a speedometer, Chaz flashes five fingers twice to indicate we're going fifty-five. This is a good place to keep it till the motor's broken in, and I drop my guard, all of my launch anxiety, and, gradually, even my phobia about loose bolts and flying front-end parts. The Flyer feels heavy, torquey, smooth-riding. The curious-looking "girder" front fork, with its coil springs and single shock, was so complex-looking to me that I resisted taking it apart until I absolutely had to. But I've replaced all the bushings and bearings, straightened it on a sheet-metal press, and now it's rock solid and sucks up the bumps like a vacuum.

I now believe that if there is a rapture of the depths, there is a rapture of the highway, too, and in a few more miles I don't care how fast I'm going. I don't care about much of anything, as long as we can keep moving like this forever.

I'm out here doing fifty-five under the most unlikely of circumstances—on a machine of my own creation. To describe this as a leap of faith does not begin to do it justice. For a man of my mechanical abilities, it is more in the realm of foolhardiness, yet here I am: the guy that installed the lifters in his Chevy upside down. The guy who ran his buddy's English Ford out of gas, and refueled it from what turned out to be a water jug. The guy who tried to fix the alternator bracket on his GMC with a Pabst can and an old flip-flop.

The miles slip by and the Flyer hangs together. And what's more, the Flyer is out there looking good. The oncoming cyclists wave, and from the corner of my eye I see a couple turn for a second look, and I suddenly see that what we're dealing with is a sterling example of one's present defeating one's past. I didn't give up on this bike, and now it's running down the highway. I didn't give up on a family, and now I've got Caroline and Phoebe. Sara, too. We'll see where it takes me with Kyle. . . .

We continue to catch all the greens, cruise along through the lights of Lolo, and we don't stop until Chaz and Yvonne pull over for directions at the Cantina LaCosina outside of Stevensville.

Chaz and Bummy are immediately all over my Chief, which sits baking to the tink of heated metal, the scent of burning Valvoline. They are looking for leaks and loose parts, and I put on my glasses and join them. The three of us crawl around in the dirt, peer up at the oil lines, peer down at the ignition wires, peer askance at the notoriously fallible Indian battery tie-down system. We don't look up till we hear the sound of Harleys pulling in close.

The woman is bare-armed, sleek-looking. She wears a black deerskin vest, fingerless demi-gloves, a Harley-Davidson turban, and beneath it her hair is sucked back so tightly it gives the impression of a discount face-lift. She's pretty in a dangerous, diamondback rattler kind of way, and she and the guy with her are both on Shovelheads.

Chaz looks up and grins. "Hey, Jimmy. What's happening?"

"Hey, Chaz," says Jimmy. "Not much at all."

Jimmy peers through his mirror shades at my Chief for what seems like several minutes before he finally says anything. By this point I am prepared to field a compliment, simply because that's the way it's gone so far. But when Jimmy finally speaks, he says, "So what's holding that front brake cable on?"

It's hard to figure what he means, but I shrug and say, "That bolt right there, I guess."

Jimmy squints, hoists a foot up on a highway peg. He shakes his head and says, "Man. You *really* cooked those brand-new pipes, didn't you?"

I look at my pipes. Well, this is true. I'd left Missoula with the chrome bright and virginal. They are a mottled orange and blue, from the header pipe all the way out to the muffler. But now I'm thinking, OK, Jimmy. Now let's have a look at *your* ride. Let's see: bob-job fenders, one primered, one rusty. A Barbarian springer front-end that's straight out of the '70s and some stubby-ass drag pipes. Jimmy's bike looks a notch past rough. I can't imagine what I'll gain by pointing this out, but I'm starting to feel I might have to anyway.

Yvonne returns from Cantina LaCosina and defuses things—she greets the lady Shovel rider cordially, they both fire up a Marlboro, and the two are suddenly immersed in a conversation about the nutritional benefits of brown rice. But more than anything, I start to want these people *gone,* so Jimmy won't be a witness to my kick-start technique.

Suddenly Yvonne is agitated, and I wonder if it's her medication. We've got exactly two hours, she says, and she's worried that the baby was too cranky, worried that the sitter will be pissed. I glance to my wrist, even though my watch strap broke early in the summer. I realize that while all summer long I've been winging it, Yvonne has restored my sense of time with a vengeance.

Do I stall the bike when I pull out? Probably. I can't remember for sure. But by this point I can put up with nearly any kind of ignominy in order to get back on that highway.

We boom along for the next few miles with me in the lead, then Chaz and Yvonne blow past. I begin to hear my motor pop, stagger, and backfire. I flip down the reserve-tank valve, but things don't improve. I grope around on the left to see if the choke is closed, and it is. The motor keeps breaking up. I pull over onto a Texaco apron just as Chaz and Yvonne disappear around the bend a half mile ahead. Bummy follows me in on the Sportster. Before I've even come to a stop, I realize I've failed to fully advance the spark. I remedy this but stall the bike twice trying to reenter traffic. The tension, the time-line business has got me flustered, and I find I'm beginning to worry about things again. Was that a rattle from the steering head? A shimmy in the front fork? How late *are* we, anyway? In the course of these ruminations, I overshoot our turnoff. Bummy comes streaking past me on the Sportster, waves his hand off to the west, and I nod.

I dive off the highway onto a dirt road half a mile past the turnoff, and it's just a bad spot, pitched steeply away from the pavement into heavy gravel, and it's hard to hold the bike at that angle while we wait. The traffic is solid, the gravel road is steep, and I have to cross two lanes. Bummy gets off to help me launch, but I still stall it once. Twice. Bummy jumps on the back, kicks it over with me still on it. Again I have a brief, fleeting sense of mortification that is gone almost immediately. By the time we get a window again I rev way too high in a moment of panic, stomp the clutch with my heel, and in a hail of gravel shoot out onto the highway like a rocket. The rear wheel breaks loose on the gravel, arcs out ninety degrees to the east. Instinctively I drop my foot to stabilize, and the rear tire chirps as the big bike rights itself. I never let up on the gas, push myself out of the skid almost before I know what's happened, and the Flyer is now powering off down the road under heavy throttle, me hanging on for all I'm worth.

This has a peculiar effect—it's happened too fast for me to even get scared. I feel a sense of abandon, and now I really give myself up to this ride.

Yvonne and Chaz are waiting for us back at the St. Mary's turnoff, and before I have a chance to think, I tap the brake, heel the bike over, give it throttle, and dart across the highway in front of a Cherokee wagon.

The road turns to gravel in half a mile, and I probably should shift to a lower gear, but as I pass Chaz he gives me a look of what I take for genuine admiration as I go whizzing past. I know what he's thinking: It's crazy to ride so fast in this gravel, but as the sun ricochets off the snow-fields of the Bitterroot, it strikes me that the gravel roads of the Depression era were exactly the kind of road the Flyer was built for in the first place.

Now Chaz is in the lead as we come up fast on a piece of survey flagging a couple miles ahead. This time it's his turn to overshoot, since I'm able to stop just a few yards past it. I drop a leg and am about to wheel the Chief around when Bummy comes up hard on the right, hugs the ditch, and flashes by me like a comet—missing my leg by inches. He'd just come over the rise, into our dust cloud, and hadn't seen me till he was on top of me. Saved again! I feel terrific now, and it makes me recall the old Churchill adage: There's nothing more exhilarating than being shot at and missed.

We reconnoiter with Chaz and Yvonne, roll down the steep driveway, and kill the motors. I didn't know exactly where we were going when I signed on, but as it turns out, we're barbecuing at a genuine log cabin in the woods. There is a drift boat on a trailer and a Harley Heritage special parked in a lean-to.

We're greeted by Rob, a wiry, bearded guy in his late forties who works for Plum Creek Timber. Rob looks at my Flyer, which is sitting there smoking from an oil seep in the hot Labor Day sun. Rob shakes his head and says, "Man. That is a thing of beauty. . . ."

Rob has an easy, self-effacing humor. I'm immediately comfortable with him, and we sit out on his deck, drink a Wicked Ale, and I begin to unwind.

I'm thinking about how it's the last day of summer, the last day of the full moon. It's about a year, give or take a month, from when I dragged the various chunks of this bike home on the bed of my truck, shoved them to the back of my garage in a big rusty pile. And now here I am, I've gone thirty some miles down the Bitterroot Valley, and I haven't wrecked the Flyer yet!

I have another swig of Wicked Ale. Of course, I still have to make it home. But sitting out on this wonderful deck among the Douglas firs and pines, the smell of conifers rises like incense in the heat. Chaz embarks on the subject of chain saws, and while these guys are murmuring along I'm thinking, Wow. Why don't *I* have a place like this?

Because, I tell myself, I can't *afford* one. I spent all my money on this frigging motorcycle.

I finish my ale. The back deck is filling up with friends and family and a couple of little girls who want to toast their hot dogs. I think that in a couple of summers my own little girl may be out here with them. Although I go back and forth on this topic a lot, today I decide that life is good.

Before the hamburgers are cooked, Yvonne becomes restless. She is swigging Coke, pacing and prowling. There is something about a phone call to be made, something about the sitter, and then suddenly we all need to go. It's too bad, because I decide I really *want* a burger now. I can't remember if I ate breakfast or not, and I'm starved.

Gassing up on the way home, I unintentionally lay a three-foot patch of rubber coming out of the Mini Mart, and it leaves Chaz and Bummy in hysterics. Running by the university in the homestretch, an old friend spots me, waves, and toots his horn. When I part company with the Harleys, I have a chance to really study the Flyer. It sits cooking in the drive, 50-weight Valvoline dripping from two or three different places, but I don't care—I'll fix it later. The chain grease spattered around my rear whitewall forms a kind of biker's mandala, and as Jimmy pointed out, my chrome pipes are now nicely oxidized. As for me, my right foot is swollen from all the cranking I've done, and when I peer in the rearview mirrors, I see that I'm windburned, that my hair is blown around into a modified Don King. There is no ceremony, no group urination or anything like that, but I realize things have changed. I feel cocky with the Flyer now. I feel *blooded.*

CHAPTER 22

STURGIS AND BEYOND

IT'S MONTHS BEFORE I LEARN TO RIDE THE FLYER CLEANLY. THE foot clutch and left-hand throttle continue to baffle me, and by the end of October I've probably stalled the Flyer at every major intersection in town. What's more, until I overhaul my charging system and figure out the gas mileage, pushing the big bike home is an all-too-familiar exercise. Once, when the Flyer and I were laboring along, huffing and puffing, an older woman in sweatpants and running shoes crossed the street to talk to me.

"Out of gas?" she says.

"No," I tell her. "I think it's a dead battery. This time, at least."

"Oh," she says. "That's a shame. It certainly is *pretty*, your motorcycle. I don't believe I've ever heard of an Indian before."

I tell her I wish I'd never heard of one either, then I push the Flyer on back to my shop for another evening of troubleshooting.

Still, everywhere we go, the Flyer provokes responses that range from curiosity to admiration to outright lust, and more than once the bike receives wolf whistles while I'm waiting at the light. This particular response is at once the most gratifying and the hardest to deal with, and I haven't yet figured out my reply, other than to assume the worst kind of false modesty — "What, *this* old thing?" And yet when the Flyer goes unnoticed, I get cranky and petulant.

Sometime in November, I put my Indian away for the winter. I remove the battery, drain the carburetor, and roll it into the back of my garage, where it sits—low, dark, and shiny—behind the most recent stack of papers and beer bottles.

Chaz's tools are still scattered around—his torch and wrenches, a coffee can full of oil-line fittings, and the odd chunks of Indian Joe we didn't cannibalize for my rear brakes. The chrome side stand I never bought—I opted for a black one—is still here, as well as the ten-toothed kick lever Chaz first sold me, then later replaced with the correct, twelve-tooth version. There is also a scuba diver's speargun, some shaky-looking sheet-metal storage racks, and a plastic bag of sleeveless T-shirts, all size XXL—the kind of debris I've come to know as Chaz's spoor.

It looks like some peculiar fusion experiment took place here, and in fact, it did. The end product—the transformation of a machine with its best years behind it into a machine for the future—took the best of Chaz, the best of his parts pile, and the best of me, too. In much the same manner that he lives his life, our friendship would veer dangerously close to the edge, only to right itself at the last possible moment. Mostly, like some mythical trickster, Chaz was maddening and flighty, yet deadly serious when it mattered most, and every time we reached a point of no return, he came through with virtuoso displays of ingenuity and tenacity: his touch with the rusted shackle bearings, his eye with the bent front end tree, his call on the misaligned intake manifold, to name a few. Then there was Shane with his circuit tester, and Sneezy, who showed me how to wire my handlebars. There was Speedstick, who aligned all the motor mounts; Bummy, who showed me how to trim my fenders; Kevin, who helped so often and so willingly. There was Manny and Cowboy Bob with their stories, and my old friends Bryan, Kim, and Neil, who don't know any more about motorcycles than I do, but who were up for just about anything. And of course, Rick, Ronnie, and Magoo, whose work on this bike will shine on into the next century.

In the end, the project I envisioned as a solitary one became a wild skunk works collaborative that ended up involving the skills of a whole community of artisans, craftsmen, and friends, a project that had us all fixing, fabricating, and scavenging parts in a sweaty back-alley garage. Essentially, we ended up doing all the things that Hank Beckwith, with his pronouncements, self-aggrandizements, and sanitized top-dollar outfit swears you'll never catch him doing. Yet these improvisations are the heart of the tradition of the backyard Daedalus that stretches back for centuries.

When we first found out about Phoebe, I wondered if these two enterprises, the baby and the motorcycle, could actually run parallel. At some point I wondered, jokingly, why there were no men arriving with motorcycle parts, as there were women with maternity wear. But over and over, at all times of the day and night, a group of men *did* show up in my garage, offering their time and energy to this restoration, for no other reason but the love of it. In a way, what holds this restless, disparate, and sometimes troubled group of men together is what holds the Flyer together, too. Perhaps that's what people are actually seeing when they stop to admire it—that the Flyer is a kind of incarnation of the best qualities we all had to offer.

At one point Caroline said it was like having a garden made up of cuttings from the gardens of your friends. Maybe she's right. What's more, the patience, humor, focus, and invention practiced in that garage are exactly the skills I'll need to raise young Phoebe, who I fully expect will bring out the best in me, too.

Maybe with these skills I can take a muddled fifty-two-year-old, obsessed with his failures and the failures of his father, and turn him into a man who has patience, forbearance, and understanding—turn him into a good father who finds delight in his child.

New Year's comes and goes, and once again I miss the Montana Legends Annual Ride, but only because I was on the way back from Washington, D.C., reeling from a couple of startling events. After climbing trees the last four years, I had my first Modern Language Association job interviews since I left California. Suddenly it was time to change costumes again, and I left my Wellingtons and greasy Levi's at home, wore a pair of Haggar slacks, the requisite tweed jacket, and the first pair of oxford shoes I've owned in twenty-five years.

On the evening of my last interview, Phoebe and Caroline and I met my daughter Sara in a Georgetown restaurant, and when I walked in, there sat the grinning Kyle, returned to my waking world for the first time in twenty-two years.

Like the night I started up the Flyer, the rest of the evening was dreamscape. Kyle and I talked amiably while Sara sat across from us, fussing with the baby and watching. We talked about the West, about basketball, about cars. Kyle seemed to bear no grudge. Perhaps he's found, as I have, that this fatherhood business and all its expectations are convoluted and confusing, and that sometimes it's just easier to let it all slide.

I try not to stare, but it's hard. Kyle is charming, athletic, a good-looking guy who appears not the least bit inclined to spend the next twenty-five years of his life testing the laws of gravity or any other kind of laws, for that matter. He seems like a young man of whom any father would be proud. At one point he sneaks a look, catches me sneaking a look at him. We both know what it means: Who *are* you?

All the way home I think about that evening—the deep-purple nail polish our waitress wore, the way Sara looks as a bottle blonde. The babaganoush, the Anchor Steam beers, the peach sorbet, and that frantic old Robert Palmer song they kept playing, the one I knew the name of but couldn't place. The company of Caroline and three lovely children made it all seem miraculous, but I can't figure out what to make of it, what it means. Somewhere, flying out of Minneapolis with my third bag of peanuts and Phoebe in my lap, I see it didn't mean anything, much beyond the fact that we were all there for that moment, all five of us together. I wonder if the chance to know Kyle has already come and gone. I wonder if the chance will ever present itself for me to let Kyle know that I've missed him. Mostly, I wonder if I have been like my own father, who I now understand is terribly afraid of letting me know the man he suspects he is—a man who has nothing to give.

In the summer of '97, Chaz struggles to finish a brutish 100ci "Pro-Street" custom Harley-Davidson in time to ride it to Sturgis with me. He pumps thousands of dollars into it, but like the year before, he falls short, runs out of money and time.

Yvonne left him sometime in June. Whether she's gone for a few months or gone forever, nobody seems to know for sure. Mostly, Chaz carries this gracefully, but there is a resignation in him I have not seen before. Bummy's wife was killed on the interstate in July, and a few weeks later he broke his leg in a bar fight. Sneezy never finished the Knucklehead he planned to ride to Sturgis this year—he fell in love over the summer and never looked back. Magoo was too busy. Manny Madrid said, "Know what? There's too damn many *people* at that thing." In the end, I head out for Sturgis alone. In a way, I'm not surprised.

On a Thursday morning I leave my motel in Gillette, Wyoming, don my leathers, check my gas, and fire up the Flyer. We're in the high plains at 6,000 feet. It's been a wet summer in the Rockies, and the countryside is soft and green as spring. It's funny how small the bike seems, how the 80ci motor sounds almost tinny in these vast stretches.

I warm it up a moment, pull down my goggles, and pop it in gear, prepare for the final lap of a journey that began over two years before, in the back of my garage.

Out on the interstate, the Flyer is running strong. Before I left, I removed a Chaz-rigged spark advance bracket so the motor could run at full advance instead of seven-eighths. And embarrassingly I discovered that, for whatever reason, I'd been riding with my tires at about half inflation all summer. Now the Flyer feels solid, powerful, and agile, and the song of the big V-twin never wavers.

When you ride a fifty-year-old motorcycle, you take it easy. Since I don't have a working speedometer, I estimate my speed by the sound of the motor. With my twenty-four-tooth sprocket, sixty to sixty-five mph is the quietest ride in the power band, the "sweet spot." I know I can ride at seventy and maybe more, but I like the idea that my oil stays cool enough for me to leave my hand on the tank. I've brought along a pressurized can of Fix-a-Flat and a couple of open-end wrenches, and when I think of what I carried with me my first time out, I have to laugh. If I ever fell in the river with that kind of hardware, I'd go straight to the bottom.

I'm booming along nicely when an Evolution Harley comes up from behind, traveling so fast I never even see it. As he blows past, the rider does a double take, drops back to pace me, swerves in close for a better look. At sixty-five miles per hour, we're about two feet apart, and I crowd the shoulder and try to keep my eyes on the road while he studies my bike, nose to tail, like some kind of centerfold. He's sunburned and stubble-faced, with a Jolly Roger do-rag bound tight to his skull. He shakes his head, grins wolfishly. "Fuckin' *COOL!*" he shouts over the roar of our bikes, then he grabs a handful and is off down the road like a shot.

By Sundance, with seventy miles to go, the biker traffic picks up. The big Harleys travel seventy to seventy-five, and when they pass me I get the thumbs-up. At one point a van passes, slows, and the passenger hangs out the window to wave me down. Instantly I'm paranoid again, think I'm dropping parts, but then she brandishes a camera. She wants me to pull in close for a better shot. The Millennium Flyer, it turns out, is a hit.

The Vintage Bike Rally is in Rapid City this year, and I stop in Sturgis just to gas up. The bike traffic is like an anthill. It takes me ten minutes just to make it to a gas pump, and I get back on the road as soon as possible, eager to get to Rapid City.

I find the Vintage Bikes easily, nose the Flyer through a hole in the barricades, and immediately a man comes up and says, "Park it by the curb. Grab a ticket, fill it out, attach it to the handlebar." Then he's gone.

I sit on my bike for a moment, deflated. The guy has all the charm and enthusiasm of a parking-lot attendant with a bad hangover. My vanity is wounded. I'm still pouting as I back the Flyer into the curb and fill out my tag, but then I'm converged upon by a couple of enthusiasts—a guy from Iowa, who wants to know about my charging system, and a middle-aged fellow from Minnesota with a peculiar look in his eye. I study him for a moment. I *know* that look. I know the way he paws through the souvenir T-shirts and hats, the way he dogs all the Indian owners and pumps them for information. He is about to buy himself a basketcase, and in his terrible earnestness he reminds me quite a bit of myself about twenty-six months back. In a way, I envy him this. And in another way, I do not.

"Have you got any advice to pass on?" he asks me finally.

"Yes," I tell him. "One: If you buy a basket, buy a Chief.

"Two: Learn to accept the 5–10 Law; spend five thousand dollars initially, and it will cost you another ten thousand. Or maybe twelve thousand. Or thirteen thousand.

"Three: Don't buy a basketcase. They are pigs in pokes. They will break your heart. They will drive you mad."

I'm restless in Rapid City. I go through a nearby gallery, go up the street to the microbrewery, where I have a Chukkar Ale and a bowl of buffalo soup. By the time I get back to the rally, more bikes have arrived, including several vintage Harleys and a nifty pre-unit Triumph. There are a number of Indians that I remember from the '95 Rally, and as I study their cad-plated bolts, oil-free cases, and pristine exhaust pipes, I finally understand, firsthand, that there are two kinds of Indian motorcycles: the riders and the show bikes. Out of the twenty to thirty Indians at the rally, only the Flyer and a couple of others had been ridden any distance. It was clear that the rest of them were brought in on trailers.

By the time the contestants line up for the plank race and kick-start contest, I've had enough. I'm tired of talking about Indians. I'm even tired of looking at them. It's a beautiful late-summer afternoon, and more than anything I want to get back on the road. And with that I start the Flyer up, ride through the concourse, and head for the Interstate and the long ride back to Gillette.

Seventy miles out, it's going on four and I'm thirsty. I dive off the highway at Sundance, head for the bar with a line of Harleys thirty bikes long. I cruise the row, choose a parking spot, and dismount while a dozen bikers watch from sidewalk tables.

"Partner," says the first biker I encounter, "your scoot is just plain *beautiful*."

I have a beer, and then the bartender buys me one. I want a shot of bourbon, too, but I'm too smart for that. It's an exhilarating afternoon for me here in the wild heart of the Rockies. Several of us sit out front and admire the day, the bikes, and the country. It is an easy yet intimate kind of fellowship. The beer is cold, Bob Seger is singing a song called "Katmandu," and the afternoon is long, warm, languorous. I have to try hard not to let my eyes rest upon it too fondly, because soon enough it's time to go.

I stroll out to the Flyer, fire it up, and wave so long to my new friends. I know that in restoring this Indian I've done something enigmatic, mysterious. It's one of those things that make no sense at all, but at the same time it makes all the sense in the world, and I ride off with a sense of possibility. Fuckin' *COOL*.

And somewhere between Rozet and Wyodak, the last twenty miles to Gillette, as the traffic thins out and the wind blows hard against my goggles, I grab a handful of throttle and the big bike leaps ahead. Wyoming blows past me in a great rush of heat, light, and summer-scented air as the Flyer and I ride hard for home.

EPILOGUE

"Never sell your bike, Stroker.
The bills come and go, but you sell
that bike and it's gone for good." CHAZ

THE 5-10 LAW NOTWITHSTANDING, THIS PROJECT I BEGAN ON $5,000 mad money in June of '95 ended up costing me slightly over $17,000. The unforeseen expenses (like a new $500 wheel, a $700 tank rebuild, and $400 S&S flywheels) along with numerous express shippings and blind alleys (the rebuild on a wheel I never used, a bad battery I had to absorb, and a twelve-volt generator I scrapped for an alternator), plus dozens of long-distance calls for technical help, all took their toll. But mostly, I finished this project with an appreciation for the real cost of these machines—for the way biker families must learn that the promise these old motorcycles hold out is strong enough to preempt nearly anything.

Yvonne's been gone six months now. Chaz is smoking again, and divorce seems imminent. Yet for all the acrimony I saw between these two, Chaz struggles terribly with these developments. For all I know,

Yvonne does, too. Certainly they are flawed. Mostly they are good and generous people who have a real knack for bringing out the worst in each other, and I thank my lucky stars for Caroline and Phoebe, who seem so effortlessly to bring out my best.

Phoebe is nearly two now. She'll be two and a half when her baby brother arrives in the spring, and I'm told this is a good spacing. The other day I bought her a Big Wheel tricycle and she studied it for a moment, climbed up on the seat, and jumped down hard on it. Then she did it again. I looked at Caroline, curious. "What in the world is she doing?"

"I think," said Caroline, "she's trying to kick-start her trike."

I still haven't found a teaching job, though last year I made it to the finals. Mostly I've stopped worrying about it, and with the century about to roll over, Chaz and I still work in the trees. He gets on my nerves sometimes, but I am careful to keep on his good side. I'll need all the help I can get from him when I start work on the 1941 45ci basketcase I just bought from him—the one lying in the back of my garage, next to the Millennium Flyer. When Phoebe's of age, it will be small enough for her to start by herself, fast enough to keep up with me.

ABOUT THE AUTHOR

Fred Haefele has taught creative writing at the University of Montana and Stanford, where he held a Jones Lectureship. He has received fellowships from the NEA, the Fine Arts Work Center in Provincetown, and Sewanee University. Currently, he works as an arborist, and lives in Montana with his wife and two children.